"In The Beginning God Created...

The Country Church"

The Miracle at Marion, Texas

By Pastor Butch Ikels

Resource Publications
An imprint of Wipf and Stock Publishers
Eugene, Oregon

Resource Publications
An imprint of Wipf and Stock Publishers
199 West 8th Avenue, Suite 3
Eugene, OR 97401

In The Beginning God Created...
The Country Church
Copyright©2005 by Butch Ikels
ISBN: 159752-092-6
Publication Date: February 2005

10   9   8   7   6   5   4   3   2   1

Contents

About the Author

Elton "Butch" Ikels was born on August 22, 1945 and then born again on September 9, 1963. Butch's mother died when he was 6 years old. Her deathbed request to his father was that Butch and his sister be taken to church. His father, though working seven days a week in car sales, was faithful in keeping that request.

The church Butch was raised in was both liturgical and lethargic. In his senior year of high school, God sent a faithful witness to share His simple plan of salvation with Butch. Through this witness and upon hearing the faithful preaching of God's Word, Butch came to a saving knowledge of the Lord Jesus Christ. (He later married the witness – Joan Fox!)

God blessed Butch and Joan Ikels with two precious children, Keith and Melissa, their spouses Annette and Mark, and five "grand" children: Derrick, Kristie, Amber, Danyelle, and Nathan.

Before surrendering in 1977 to God's call to preach, Butch spent 15 years in the grocery industry working as a truck driver, salesman, management and finally as a director of marketing. In January of 1978, he was called to serve as Pastor of Salem Sayers Baptist Church in Adkins, Texas (outside of San Antonio). This church averaged one baptism per week for 15 years and saw the budget increase 600 percent.

In January of 1993, Butch entered full-time evangelism. He served the Lord in this manner for five years learning lessons on God's faithfulness that are invaluable still today. In March of 1998, God created *The Country Church*. *The Country Church* was truly a modern miracle, given by God to confound the wise and comfort the afflicted. To God be all glory and honor and praise in His church.

What Others Say About the Author

Elton 'Butch' Ikels is one of the most colorful human beings I have ever known. His incredible successes in the business world make it almost certain that if Pastor Ikels had not had his life radically changed by the second birth and a call to ministry, he would probably be today one of the wealthiest ranchers in all of the earth. With his pension for fun and his beguiling sense of humor, he would have been a lark to be around. How grateful to God I am today that rather than using all of those talents and abilities selfishly and for business, he dedicated them to the Lord and became the founding pastor of *The Country Church* in Marion, Texas. What comes through in <u>God Created the Country Church</u> is the driving compassion of a man's heart to see others come to Christ coupled with an earnest conviction that all pretenses need to be laid aside and that integrity needs to be practiced by the church of God. This integrity of heart committed to missions and evangelism Butch Ikels has modeled in one of the most unique churches of which I am aware. I commend this volume to you as an example of how such should be done.

Paige Patterson,
President Southwestern Baptist Theological Seminary, Fort Worth, Texas

In an age obsessing over "non-traditional" this and "cutting-edge" that, Butch Ikels and *The Country Church* innovate the old-fashioned way. They love Jesus and they love people, they preach and teach the Bible, and they do church simply and unpretentiously. This story needs telling for a hundred reasons—but not least to remind all of us, pastors and professors and people in the pew, that the greatest need anybody has ("felt" or not) is Jesus Christ.

C. Richard Wells,
Senior Pastor, South Canyon Baptist Church, Rapid City, South Dakota
Former President, Criswell College, Dallas, Texas

The Country Church is indeed a miracle! Jesus is the miracle worker. Pastor Butch Ikels is merely the vessel used by the Lord to bring about the miracle. The Lord is always looking for a willing vessel to whom He can implant a vision; someone who is not filled with himself, nor seeking self-glory. Butch Ikels is such a person.

It took Butch over 25 years to "unlearn" how to do church the "traditional way" and start doing church the "Jesus way". The result is *The Country Church* of Marion, Texas.

To watch a thousand people from unchurched backgrounds flow through its doors is a testimony to God's love for the lost and to Butch's heart to reach them with the Gospel.

I count Butch Ikels a friend and a fellow harvester of souls.

Dr. R. Alan Streett,
Professor of Evangelism, Criswell College, Dallas, Texas

"In the Beginning God Created The Country Church," is a unique book about a unique church with a very unique pastor. Butch Ikels is a pastor that has a heart to reach people for the Lord Jesus Christ. I have known Butch since 1978, and he has always had the same call on his life, reaching people for Jesus! Take time to read carefully what has gone on in this unique church, but take a little more time to read between the lines and see the absence of a church bureaucracy, the heart of a pastor, and the freshness of God's anointing.

Brother Dennis Spire, Pastor, Calvary Baptist Church, San Marcos, Texas

The Lord Jesus has placed within the heart of Butch Ikels a simple emphasis of ministry: calling out men, women, boys and girls to receive the Lord Jesus as their personal Savior. He is wise enough to know his calling and trusts the Lord for what he will need to obey that call.

The "Country Church" concept was given by our Lord to fill the need of honest seekers who were turned off by the elaborate "trappings" of too many of our evangelical churches today. The fellowship is so genuine that people you thought would never come to church regularly are greeting people at the door each Sunday morning and Thursday night.

Having been his friend for 35 years, I know Butch to be a humble servant of Christ Jesus. I rejoice in what our Lord is doing in this supernatural movement of His Spirit.

Brother Neil Kibbe, Pastor, Comal Country Church, New Braunfels, Texas

After years of experience both as a successful pastor and evangelist, Butch Ikels was frustrated by the lack of evangelistic effectiveness that he witnessed in the typical Southern Baptist church. Instead of focusing upon the Kingdom of God, he observed that churches were focused upon "doing" church. Evangelism and church planting were, at best, an after-thought and often viewed to be threatening to the welfare of the existing congregation.

In a bold move of faith, Brother Butch determined to start a church that would be "different." He has succeeded in accomplishing that goal. *The Country Church* is different!

The Country Church is different because by its very organization and structure, the typical, often controversial, activities that consume so much of the membership's time and energy is unnecessary at *The Country Church*. Most pastors and church leaders will excitedly search this book to discover that secret alone.

The Country Church is different in that there is a determined effort to stifle pretence at *The Country Church* – the attendee is free to be real, both in appearance and at heart. Brother Butch emphasizes dressing-down – no ties. As a result, you see all kinds of apparel in attendance. It is a visible expression of the freedom that exists in the Spirit of God as described in 2 Corinthians 3:17.

As you read his story, you will not only be blessed, but you will be challenged to also step out in faith. May God raise up many who, like Brother Butch, will determine to make a difference for the Kingdom of God before the Master of the Kingdom returns.

Dr. J.K. Minton,
Director of Missions, Blue Bonnet Baptist Association, New Braunfels, Texas

Acknowledgments

The people who have encouraged, inspired, and assisted me are legion. Some have assisted me directly and others indirectly.

To my beloved helpmate, "Mrs. Joanie", I owe more than life itself. She is my love and joy who has encouraged me almost forty-one years.

To my children and grandchildren who have given me untold blessings. They have brought me pride and never a moment's grief.

To the wonderful family of *The Country Church,* its staff and co-laborers, without whom any of this would be possible.

To Dr. Paige Patterson, President of Southwestern Baptist Theological Seminary, who coaxed, convicted, prodded, and possibly even prayed that the "Miracle at Marion" (*The Country Church*) be chronicled for future generations.

To Dr. R. Alan Streett, Professor of Evangelism at Criswell College, who not only has given me great insight, but is a brother beloved who has "been there, done that and bought the T-shirt."

To Dr. C. Richard Wells, former President of Criswell College, and now pastor of the South Canyon Baptist Church in Rapid City, South Dakota with whom I first shared *The Country Church* vision. After prayer, it was decided that depending on what happened, one year later I would come to the college and share the experience, or he would send money for groceries!

To my heroes in the faith: men I have listened to, learned from, and prayed for: men who have allowed themselves to be used of God to benefit those of us who labor in unknown fields in obscure places. I would like to acknowledge men like Dr. Adrian Rogers, Dr. Jerry Vines, Dr. Charles Stanley, Dr. Paige Patterson, and the late Dr. W.A. Criswell.

To the lovely Lord Jesus who loved me, saved me, and with a sense of humor, called me to preach.

Preface

My prayer is that God would use these pages to encourage and perhaps inspire preachers to seek a fresh touch from the Lord in planting a new work for the Kingdom. It is not written for the halls of academia, or for the entertainment of the intelligentsia. It is a feeble attempt of the author to persuade men that the power of God is available for the planting of new churches.

While struggling over the matter of putting this to print, I was led to the passage in *I Corinthians 1:27-31* that reads, *"But God hath chosen the foolish things of the world to confound the wise; and God hath chosen the weak things of the world to confound the things which are mighty; And base things of the world, and things which are despised, hath God chosen, yea, and things which are not, to bring to nought things that are: That no flesh should glory in his presence. But of him are ye in Christ Jesus, who of God is made unto us wisdom, and righteousness, and sanctification, and redemption: That, according as it is written, He that glorieth, let him glory in the Lord."*

May God bless you in your labors,

Elton "Butch" Ikels
Founding Pastor, *The Country Church*

Introduction

It is one thing to see a miracle; it is another thing to experience one. Some time ago, I tried to imagine what it must have been like not to just stand on the shore and watch the Red Sea parting, but to actually be one of the Israelites walking right in the middle of it looking up at the great wall of water on both sides. I think had I been there I would have wept at the awesomeness of God's power to save His people from certain death. In a very real way, God is still miraculously delivering His people and I weep with joy. Many people in Guadalupe County are being saved and we now have a glimpse of what it must feel like to witness firsthand God's miracles. To actually be a part of all this is very exciting.

It may not seem like a miracle to some, but to the folks in these parts, no other word more accurately defines what we are experiencing right now in Marion, Texas. Christians and non-Christians both agree, something extraordinary is happening in our tiny little part of South Texas.

As of this writing, *The Country Church* is averaging more people in church on Sunday than are in the entire town. Located in Guadalupe County, the population of Marion is approximately 1,100. Each Sunday morning this family of Believers has gathered together for worship and there have been approximately 1,100 of us.

Each week hundreds of people, all of them "plain ole country folk", gather in the name of King Jesus to worship, pray, hear God's Word preached in a simple, down-home fashion, and witness miracle after miracle. Dressed in blue jeans and boots, *The Country Church* members have the privilege of seeing people saved, make professions of faith, and join the church Sunday after Sunday. They get the sweet privilege of seeing friends, family, neighbors, and even total strangers giving their hearts to Jesus and being changed by the power of the gospel, and following Him as a Believer in Scriptural baptism.

Yes, I know this happens all over country, and there are congregations everywhere that get to experience the same kind of thing each week. We praise God with every congregation that knows what it is like to see someone walk the aisle and profess Christ

1

as Savior every week. But what makes this so miraculous is that we are not in a large metropolis where there are hundreds of thousands of people from which to draw.

Marion, Texas has no stoplight and very few stop signs. There is a very small city hall, several small businesses and a local bank. It is home to the Marion Bulldogs, a small 3-A school district. Except for the buildings on the campus of *The Country Church*, there has not been a building built in Marion in about 50 years that was not built with taxpayer money. The fire department is all volunteer and the mayor also operates the small, hometown grocery store. Small homes and big barns on acreage that has been passed down from generation to generation dot the land; there really is nothing out here.

In fact, seven years ago, a local association of churches who did a study of the area determined that is was not good financial stewardship and not necessary to start a church in this area. They did decide that if anything were to be done in this area, it should probably be a Hispanic mission to reach the small Hispanic population in the area. In the end, nothing was ever started in this area.

Now, let's give that vision committee credit. In a sense, they were exactly right about not starting a church in this area. If a *traditional* congregation had been formed anywhere around here, if it survived at all, more than likely it would have remained a small, struggling, bi-vocational work for many years. The truth is that the people in this area are not interested in that kind of church. There are plenty of congregations to choose from not far from our area that are made up of genuinely saved, loving, God-fearing folk. They meet each week to worship the Lord and minister to one another – but the local un-churched folk are just not interested. The signs out front say "Sunday Morning Worship 11:00 A.M. – Ya'll Come" and the people around here won't, and don't.

Yet, against all reason and without taking any credit or glory, Pastor Butch Ikels preaches each Sunday morning to over 1,000 people. That is more than the entire population of the area. People are now driving in from all over the area to be a part of The Miracle at Marion. Why? Because they get to hear a preacher with more degrees than a thermometer? Not hardly. Because the music is high church saturated with preludes and postludes from a pipe organ? No. Because the youth are uniformed and disciplined having been raised in an institutional Sunday School? No.

People come because God continues to choose *"the weak things of the world to confound the wise."* They come because there is no pretense. They come and find people loving Jesus and loving each other. They find people who have learned that worn down boots and faded jeans are not a test of true fellowship. The people who attend find a warmth and sincerity that is missing in a world of plastic.

They come for many different reasons. But one thing is for sure, they come because God is here and He is working in the lives of people Sunday after Sunday. People are experiencing God here and they just keep coming.

Wherever God is present something extraordinary is going to happen, and there is no doubt God is in Marion, Texas. Something extraordinary happens every week and we are so grateful to be a part of it.

The following account of how it all started, what is going on, and how things happen around *The Country Church* is intended to be a testimony to God's power and grace in our lives. More than anything God deserves the praise, honor and glory for what He is doing in us and through us. It is the primary reason for this book. We offer Him our praise.

But we also pray and desire that this little work will be a source of encouragement and information to you as you strive to discover God's plan for your church or ministry. The testimonies herein contain information that as you glean and apply it, we believe God will raise up more congregations to His own glory. In fact, He is already doing it, as "Country Churches" are springing up all over our area.

Where there are "country folk" there can be a Country Church. All over the nation there are people just like the people in and around Marion. They are plain ole country folk, "good ole boys and girls" with a need for the Savior and the need for their lives to be different. This is the story of how by the leadership and power of the Holy Spirit and God's great Gospel, hundreds have come to Christ, and the people in these parts are witnessing The Miracle in Marion, Texas...

...*In The Beginning, God Created The Country Church*.

Article taken from Guadalupe Valley Electric Co-op Review Magazine

Marion Church Is Growing By Leaps & Bounds

What started just a few years ago as a tiny ministry in a tiny town seems to have caught on and caught on BIG! In less than four years time, *The Country Church* has grown from a fledgling group of seven people, who met weekly at a location on Hard Luck Road, to a congregation of over 800, who now meet in their expanding building on FM78, just west of Marion.

Pastor Elton "Butch" Ikels has led the church from its beginning when he and his wife hosted a group of seven in their home. After five years as a full-time evangelist, or traveling minister, who preached overseas in Nigeria, Uganda, and Brazil, Ikels felt there needed to be a strong new ministry in Guadalupe County.

Six weeks in to the ministry, the congregation had grown to 37 and had outgrown the Ikels' home. The ministry moved to the only available building in Marion, which was a vacant bar. Over the next year-and-a-half, the congregation had grown to 160 and, again, had outgrown their meeting place.

The Country Church had purchased three acres of land, for a future building site, at 1005 FM78, 3/10 of a mile west of Marion. Construction was completed on the new church in April, 2000. Before the church was even completed, the congregation continued to grow at such a fast pace that several classrooms and a hallway had to be eliminated from the plans to accommodate the growing membership.

Since the church has experienced such phenomenal growth, an additional three acres was purchased and now, two years later, they are about to move into the 1,100 seat-capacity auditorium. One interesting point about this is that the new auditorium will seat slightly more people than actually live in Marion.

In addition to the growth of their own church, *The Country Church* has sponsored three new mission churches: The Comal Country Church in New Braunfels, The Oakwood Country Church in LaVernia, and the Spanish-speaking Zorn Country Church in Zorn.

The Country Church in Marion has a growing congregation of over 800. When asked about their extraordinary growth, Pastor Ikels said, "People are hungering for spiritual things. We have a down-home, "folksy" atmosphere. I preach in boots and jeans. Some, who might have stayed home otherwise, feel comfortable to hear a message from the word of God." He added, *"The Country Church* moves away from the pipe organ of old, to the keyboard, piano, guitar, and harmonica. We're not interested in atriums, birdbaths, and stained glass. We have a windmill out front, a buckboard on the porch, and farm implements decorating the building."

Ikels also attributes personal visitation as a key to the church's growth. According to Ikels, "Thirty minutes to an hour in the home of someone really seeking the Word produces more fruit than one year of regular church attendance."

The Country Church takes up no offerings and asks for no pledge commitments. There is a milk can for the building program and a basket at the back of the church for general offering.

The Country Church draws members for Marion, Lockhart, Floresville, Boerne, Seguin, San Antonio, and the Gonzales area. They invite all to come and see what they offer. Pastor Ikels says, *"The Country Church* is for three kinds of country people—those that were, those that are, and those that want to be."

Sunday worship begins at 10:30 AM, with a bible study at 9:15 AM. There's also a midweek service on Thursday at 7:00 PM, with sandwiches at 6:15 PM. for working people. For more information, call (830)-914-4749.

Chapter 1

The Foundation

Forward Through the Fog

In 1998, seven people approached my wife and me about the need of planting a new church in Marion, Texas. As we prayed about the possibility, several subjects (like cream) began to rise to the surface. We began with who we were as a people. One, we were all unapologetically committed to the inerrant word of Scripture. Two, we were conservative in our theology. Three, by our nature we were both friendly and folksy. We did not want to appear as something we were not. There was a desire to be real in a world of plastic.

Biblically, a picture began to appear. Several Scriptures took on new importance from a foundational perspective.

> *"For other foundation can no man lay than that is laid, which is Jesus Christ."*
> *I Corinthians 3:11*

All had to begin and end with Jesus. The church was to be His from its inception.

> *"Now therefore ye are no more strangers and foreigners, but fellow citizens with the saints, and of the household of God. And are built upon the foundation of the apostles and prophets, Jesus Christ himself being the chief corner stone. In whom all the building fitly framed together groweth unto an holy temple in the Lord: In whom ye also are builded together for an habitation of God through the Spirit." Ephesians 2:19-22*

The church needed to begin with correct doctrine. It was, and is, our desire to "preach the truth in love." Many people today are Biblically pure yet love is absent. Others emphasize a loving church without enough doctrine to wad a shotgun. *"Yea, so have I strived to preach the gospel, not where Christ was named, lest I should build upon another man's foundation:" Romans 15:20*

Much of what we see today in church growth is merely a shuffling of the sheep. When something catches fire people will gather to watch it burn. Yet the church must remember, there is no rejoicing in heaven over "He who moveth a letter" but over the lost who are saved!

Years ago, a larger church approached me about becoming their pastor. Thoughts arose in my mind as to more people, more influence, and possibly more money. The tendency was to say, "Honey, you go and pack while I pray to see if this is God's will."

During my devotional time, in the book of Joshua, God spoke these words to me,

> *"And the children of Joseph spake unto Joshua, saying, Why hast thou given me but one lot and one portion to inherit, seeing I am a great people, foras-much as the Lord hath blessed me hitherto?* **And Joshua answered them, If thou be a great people, then get thee up to the wood country, and cut down for thyself** *there in the land of the Perizzites and of the giants, if* **mount Ephraim be too narrow for thee.**" Joshua 17:14-15 God was saying to me, if there was a bigger work for me it was to be built and not inherited.*

Many a pastor and many a church wants to reap where we've not sown. My conviction is such that little happens on Sunday if little happens Monday through Saturday. *Find a need and fill it!* This has been a successful philosophy for many individuals and businesses through the years. On the other hand *Acts 19:32* describes an event where

> *"Some therefore cried one thing, and some another: for the assembly was confused: and the more part knew not wherefore they were come together."*

Perhaps Solomon said it best, *"Where there is no vision, the people perish."* Our vision was to reach the unchurched. Our primary target was men who were not at-tending church. Our thoughts were if we can reach Dad, Mom and the children will also come. Statistics show that if a child is reached you have a 3% chance of reaching the family. If a mother is reached you have a 14% chance of reaching the family. However, if a father is reached there is a 92% chance of reaching the rest of the family!

What were some obstacles, real or perceived, that needed to be overcome? In our area, the needs of the "suit and tie'ers" were already being met. What about the "boots and jeans, gun rack behind the pickup seat" crowd? It was decided there was a need for a place that was clean, but country. A place where a man could hang his hat, pick up a donut and a cup of coffee, sit with an open Bible and learn the plain, practical truths of the Word of God. As the late J. Vernon McGee said, "Where the cookies would be placed on the bottom shelf where the kids could get hold of them!"

Finding friends is a Biblical precept. *Proverbs 18:24* reads,

> *"A man that hath friends must shew himself friendly: and there is a friend that sticketh closer than a brother."*

While the church is to be friendly, Jesus reminds us,

> *"Woe unto you, when all men speak well of you!" Luke 6:26*

Somewhere along the line many churches have become fickle, fancy, and fakey, and not faithful, fruitful and friendly. Our church would have an atmosphere of "greeting and eating" or to use a more Biblical term, *koinonia*. A place that while Biblically sound, was free, fluid and fun; a place where you hated to miss a service rather than being badgered to come!

The church chooses its alignment, its association, its support group, and the group or groups that it supports. *Amos 3:3* asks,

> *"Can two walk together, except they be agreed?"*

Deuteronomy 22:10 states that

> *"Thou shalt not plow with an ox and an ass together."*

II Corinthians 6:14-15 says,

> *"Be ye not unequally yoked together with unbelievers: for what fellowship hath righteousness with unrighteousness? And what communion hath light with darkness? And what concord hath Christ with Belial? Or what part hath he that believeth with an infidel?"*

Many a mission church fails for desiring "Biblical blessings" while violating "Biblical principles". Little is much if God is in it, and a man need not sell his birthright for a bowl of porridge.

Following the Faith

Included below is a summary of our beliefs, philosophy of ministry, and a doctrinal statement. These statements are included in a booklet that is handed to all visitors prior to our visiting their homes. This allows the newcomers to know us, and enables them to formulate important questions.

IN THE BEGINNING GOD CREATED...
"THE COUNTRY CHURCH" FOR COUNTRY FOLKS

HOW IT ALL STARTED

In the Spring of 1998, seven believers came to Butch Ikels and his wife, Joan, to pray about starting a new work in the area.

After much prayer it became clear that it was truly God's will to create *The Country Church*. During the process, it became evident that it was absolutely necessary to trust, love, and encourage one another while having confidence in Pastoral leadership. Biblically, contention or strife was to be marked and not allowed to disrupt Christ's Church.

The Country Church first assembled in the Ikels' home on Hard Luck Road in Guadalupe County, outside Marion, Texas. The fellowship began to grow until 37 people showed up at the Ikels' home for Easter services! The Pastor Ikels wife strongly suggested looking for a larger building. That building turned out to be a vacant tavern, with a beer cooler in the back, bar in the front, and two fifteen-watt light bulbs before the paint-up, fix-up began!

The Lord then provided three acres of land on Highway 78 west of Marion. The land was paid for in six months. The 11,000 square-foot building that is now *The Country Church* was dedicated on April 30, 2000.

WHY WE ARE HERE

The Country Church has a four-fold mission statement. When we understand our purpose it allows all that we do to line up with our reason for being here.

I. **To Exalt Our Savior** – The Lord Jesus is to have first place in all that we do. All the praise, the honor, and the glory for what has, is, and will be done is to go to Him. As Believers, we want to be caught up in all that He is. (Philippians 3:7-10)

II. **To Evangelize Those Outside Of Christ** – While many have religion, it is God's desire that we have a personal relationship with His only Son, The Lord Jesus. People need to know how they might have this saving relationship. This is the Good News of the Gospel which we preach. (Romans 10:9-13)

III. **To Edify The Believers In Christ** – It is our desire to build up the body; to encourage in the Word, work, and will of our Lord. We pray that *The Country Church* will be the family that prays together, stays together, and lifts each other up. (John 13:34-35)

IV. **To Equip The Believers To Do The Work Of The Lord** – Jesus said, "Follow Me and I will make you fishers of men." We understand Christ's Commission to mean if we are not fishing we are not following. The Lord does not want us to be only hearers of the Word, but doers also. So it is that we seek to disciple. (Matthew 28:18-19)

WHAT WE BELIEVE

It is important that what we believe be based totally on the Word of God which is without error. (II Timothy 3:16-17)

We believe that Christ's Church is made up of those who know Him personally. The Bible uses terms such as saved, born again, regenerated, etc., to describe this relationship. (John 3:3)

We believe that those who have received Christ should follow Christ in baptism as a born-again Believer. This is not for salvation, but an act of obedience to our Lord's command and to publicly identify with His death, burial, and resurrection. The definition of baptism is to dip, immerse, or cover completely as pictured in Romans 6. While we believe in "infant dedication", there is no record of "infant baptism" in Scripture.

We believe in the observance of the Lord's Supper for His disciples. As often as we observe it, we do it in remembrance of Him. (I Corinthians 11)

We believe in both a private and public prayer and devotional life. Prayer is simply us speaking to Him, and pouring over His Word is simply allowing Him to speak to us. (II Timothy 12:1-2)

We believe in seeking to live a separate life-style. While Believers are to live in the world, we are not to be of the world. Christ should make a difference in how we live. (Romans 12:1-2)

We believe in a literal Heaven and a literal Hell. Heaven is the home for eternity to those who are in Christ. Hell is the eternal punishment for those who have rejected Christ. Immediately following physical death, or the return of the Lord, you will have either Heaven or Hell as your eternal home. (Luke 16:19-31)

We believe that the Lord's work is to be funded the Lord's way: God's people bringing Him the first-fruits, the tenth, the tithe, of what He has blessed us with. We are to give it cheerfully and consistently. We bring it to the Lord rather than send someone to collect it. A love offering is that which is given over and above God's tenth. (Genesis 28:22, Malachi 3:8-10, Luke 16:10-13, II Corinthians 9:6-8)

We believe in the Genesis account of creation, the fall of mankind in the Garden through sin, and that the way back to God the Father is through Jesus the Son having been led by the Holy Spirit.

We believe Christ is literally coming again, in the air **for** His Church, (I Thessalonians 4) and to the Earth **with** His Church. (Revelation 19)

We believe in Christ's virgin birth, sinless life, substitutionary death (He died in my place), bodily resurrection, and soon coming return.

To these we commit ourselves as Believers in *The Country Church.*

OUR METHOD OF MINISTRY

LEADERSHIP

While *The Country Church* may be unique in the method in which it ministers, we seek to follow a Biblical pattern and not violate Biblical principles.

While the Lord charges the Pastor with the oversight of His work, *Hebrews 13:7-18 reads "it is not to be done without prayer nor a violation of Biblical principles."* The church has seven Trustees who serve as an accountability group for the Pastor.

The Country Church recognizes the Biblical role of Deacons. (Since our inception our Deacons have chosen to be recognized by service rendered rather than a position held. While *The Country Church* has been blessed with a high percentage of these faithful servants, they have chosen to minister to the Body of, Believers rather than constitute a Board.

The Country Church came to a unanimous decision not to have business meeting or committee meetings. This does not mean that every opinion shouldn't be expressed. However, it is realized that one cannot receive counsel from those who are contentious.

FINANCES

The first offering received in *The Country Church* was $250. By the grace of God and the generosity and commitment of God's people, that first offering has been multiplied many times over!

Since the beginning, *The Country Church* has sought to glorify the Lord Jesus by integrity and stewardship. Every penny coming in and going out must be given account of. While personal contributions are held in confidence, a monthly accounting of income and out-go is printed and placed in the foyer each month.

It was the Church's desire to establish a very simple budget controlled by percentages. The following guidelines were established and remain in effect.

- The first ten percent of the general offering is given to missions – a large portion of which is given to Southern Baptist mission work, which is possibly the largest growing mission involvement in our world today. The remainder goes to various evangelistic ministries including local evangelists, rescue missions, benevolent ministries, Criswell College, S.B.C. Seminaries, etc.
- Twenty-five percent is set aside for building needs – this includes utilities, insurance, any debt service, remodeling, and physical plant improvements.
- Ten percent is set aside under miscellaneous – this covers literature needs, supplies, refreshments, furniture, etc.
- Fifty-five percent is set aside for staff and salaries and benefits - Since the inception of *The Country Church*, the Pastor was/is held accountable for the management of Church staff. While staff will likely increase in number and needs, this percentage will not increase.
- Love offerings and designated offerings are received and applied over the regular general offering.

OUR PROGRAM

- To Exalt our Savior takes on many forms, not the least of which is praise and worship. Phil and Ruth Ann Jewett have been blessed with a gift from God in leading out in this ministry. They will be delighted to work with you in ministering in this area. Sundays, Thursday nights and special events give opportunities for service.

- To Evangelize the body is a priority. Dr. Adrian Rogers once said, "Either we evangelize or we fossilize!" Jesus said, "If we do not fish for the souls of men, we do not follow Him in discipleship." We are either a missionary or a mission field. Much emphasis is to be placed on visitation. Monday, Tuesday, and Wednesday are set aside for visiting with "church-wide" visitation on Monday nights.

- To Edify & Equip In addition to Sunday Morning Worship, we have:

Sunday Bible Study (All Ages)	9:15 AM
Sunday Worship (Nursery & Children's Church)	10:30 AM
Monday Nights (Church-Wide Visitation)	7:00 PM
Tuesday Night (Women's Bible Study)	7:00 PM
Tuesday Night (Men's Visitation, Devotional, Work Projects)	7:00 PM
Wednesday Morning (Women's Bible Study)	9:30 AM
Thursday Night Services (6:30 Fellowship)	7:00 PM
Thursday Night Country Kids (Nursery-5th)	7:00 PM
Thursday Night Youth	7:00 PM

Our Youth Leaders stand ready for guidance, growth, and counsel for our junior high and high schoolers.

It is desirous that each Believer be equipped to serve. Every class, every event should have this as its goal: to encourage, energize and equip the Believer for service to the Savior.

Mission trips and opportunities are to be provided on a regular basis.

OUR GOAL

Our goal is simply to seek to reach our world for Christ. We are to be passionate rather than passive, militant rather than mundane, fervent rather than flippant, and faithful rather than fancy.

As you have read this please pray for us that the Lord would choose the simple to *"confound the wise"*. *I Corinthians 1:27-31*

HOW CAN YOU BE A PART OF *THE COUNTRY CHURCH*

One, be sure that you are saved. (whether *The Country Church* is part of God's plan for you or not).

If you are not saved, why not pray something like this: "Dear Jesus, I realize that I am a sinner. I ask you to come into my heart and save me. I thank you for saving me Jesus."

Two, go public with your profession. During the invitation time at the end of service, share your decision with the Pastor.

Three, follow the Lord's command and identify with Christ's death, burial and resurrection by Scriptural baptism as a Believer.

Or, if the above has happened to you, come by a statement or a letter from a church of like faith or order.

God bless you! If we can be of any assistance or answer any questions concerning the above, please call or write:

The Country Church
1005 W. FM78
P.O. Box 421 (Mailing)
Marion, TX 78124
(830) 914-4749

"And I searched for a man among them who should build up the wall and stand in the gap before me for the land, that I should not destroy it." Ezekiel 22:30

Chapter 2

The Fears

When God opens a door of opportunity we can be assured the devil will cast fear in our face. Many have mistakenly seen an open door as an absence of obstacles! Paul wrote in *I Corinthians 16:9,*

> *"For a great door and effectual is opened unto me, and there are many adversaries."*

Some fears we feel and see. Such was the case with Peter and the wind and waves. Other fears are perceived; nevertheless, they all must be dealt with. It is not my attempt to magnify the negatives and minimize the positives, but to openly identify them that they might be dealt with.

One fear is the *fear of inadequacy.* Moses doubted his ability to reach, teach and nurture. Jeremiah feared the faces of the people. Someone once said, "God doesn't need our ability, just our availability." An old preacher friend, Brother J.O. Folkes, once asked me, "Who would God not use that was willing to be used?" Jack Taylor said, "I used to have an inferiority complex when it came to the things of God until I realized it wasn't a complex at all, I was just plain inferior!"

In Isaiah's temple experience he looked up, he looked in, and he looked out. When he looked up he saw the Lord. When he looked in he saw his inadequacy. When he looked out he saw the people who need the Lord.

The second fear is a *fear for finances.* The temptation for the church planter is to seek a secure position, with a secure salary. He may question, Lord, if this doesn't work, these people still have their jobs and homes. What about me? How will I feed my family?

A former secretary had a poster that hung over her desk. It was a picture of kittens playing in a basket. One kitten hung by a claw from the handle of the basket. Underneath the picture was this caption: Faith isn't faith until it's all you are holding on to! Amen?

At *The Country Church* our first offering was $250. I shared with a dear pastor friend that my wife and I had put in $150 of it. He replied, "If you had put more in, you could have gotten more out!" As the financial needs of a new church are added to this equation, we see that Satan has an opportunity to inflict fear in the heart of the church planter. Remember, however, the Psalmist David wrote in *Psalm 37:25,*

> *"I have been young, and now am old; yet have I not seen the righteous forsaken, nor his seed begging bread."*

A third fear we would entitle *fear of faces*. Many of the Lord's choicest servants suffered from this personal contact with the living God suffering from a fear of face. Or Elijah, who truly experienced "the hour of power" fearing the face of a single woman.

Can we imagine that intimate conversation between God and the powerful prophet, Jeremiah? "Lord, I'm inexperienced, the consequences are too great, I cannot articulate or convey your Word to their ears, and I'm afraid of what the people might think!"

Move on to the New Testament and consider the coarse and common fishermen who were called to turn a world right side up for Jesus. Or we can turn and read the instruction to "timid Timothy" who had to be encouraged to do the work of an evangelist and to take a stand for Christ and the Gospel whether he feared the faces or not!

A fourth fear we could call *The Ridicule of the Redeemed*. Sometimes the brethren bring more of a sound of defeat than the devil! It can come from a pastor friend, a beloved professor, or a trusted denomination leader. Consider a situation that *Numbers 13:32,33* and *Numbers 14:1* bring to mind.

> *"And they brought up an evil report of the land which they had searched unto the children of Israel, saying, the land through which we have gone to search it, is a land that eateth up the inhabitants thereof; and all the people that we saw in it are men of a great stature. And there we saw the giants, the sons of Anak, which come of the giants: and we were in our own sight as grasshoppers, and so we were in their sight. And all the congregation lifted up their voice, and cried: and the people wept that night."*

Sometimes fear comes from the realization that it's just you and Jesus! As a boy growing up on the East Side of San Antonio, Texas, I had a dog named Shorty. Shorty was a mixed breed with a local reputation for being "death on cats". I could sound the alarm by saying, "Cat, Shorty, cat!", and Shorty would bring himself from a dead slumber to a red alert in a heartbeat! Yet someway, somehow, a scrawny, unattractive red kitten with an attitude wormed his way into Shorty's heart. This kitten did the unthinkable! He ate from Shorty's food bowl. The kitten dared to sleep in Shorty's dog box. He even licked Shorty's ears! This kitten would roam the neighborhood picking fights with battle-scarred tomcats - one hiss, one slap to the enemy's face and then one hasty exit from the battlefield to Shorty's porch with the enemy hot on his tail! Upon arrival the kitten would slide under Shorty's legs, turn to face the enemy and calmly begin to clean himself. The delight came while watching the on-rushing enemy! When the tomcat would see Shorty and hear his deep growl, he would grind gears to get it in reverse and saturate the place with his absence!

The lesson learned by the scrawny kitten was this: to depend on a power greater than his own. It was there that he found pleasure, protection, and purpose. May we do likewise!

Another *fear to face is jealousy*. If our labor is not as fruitful as another's, we may begin to find fault rather than to do the *"first works."* We say, "They have lowered the fence where any goat can get in!" We can turn inward and become isolated, realizing that there are only two great servants for God, me and thee, and I question thee! Elijah, all alone, said, "Only I am left to serve thee, Lord." God reminded him of the thousands out there who were every bit as faithful.

If our work is blessed of the Lord then oftentimes it is we who face the attack. Our ministry, methods, and motives are open to the scrutiny of both friend and foe. Case in point: In our first building program we planned an auditorium to seat three to four times our attendance. This we felt was necessary due to the numbers being saved. Because the majority of our growth was new converts we did not build debt free. This brought rebuke from a dear brother in the Lord. His charge was that we should only build what we could pay for even if it meant a considerably smaller building. One year later, with attendance running 120 percent of design, criticism of another sort arose. A very conservative pastor friend said of our church to an assembly, "If they would have had the faith, they would have built larger rather than building again one year later." Sometimes one feels like the brother who dressed in union pants and a confederate shirt. Both sides shot him to death!

Paul told the saints assembled at Rome in *Romans 12:15, "*

Rejoice with them that do rejoice, and weep with them that weep."

Possibly the church has incorporated half of this verse into our lives. We have learned to weep with those who weep, but we have not yet learned to rejoice with those who rejoice.

A dear brother in the faith, Brother Neil Kibbe, once told me, "Butch, one of the greatest steps in my Christian pilgrimage came when I realized God was using people I didn't even approve of!"

And so it is!

Chapter 3

The Faith

Most of us in Christendom have a Biblical understanding of "faith." For example, we know and believe

> *"For by grace are ye saved <u>through faith</u>; and that not of yourselves; it is the gift of God:" Ephesians 2:8*

We also agree and affirm

> *"Now faith is the substance of things hoped for, the evidence of things not seen." Hebrews 11:1*

We have read *Hebrews 11:6*

> *"But without faith it is impossible to please him; for he that cometh to God must believe that he is, and that he is a rewarder of them that diligently seek Him."*

My calling in Christ has taken me along exciting paths. From a stable, growing church for 15 years to mission trips from Nigeria to Uganda, and Mexico to Brazil. Then I spent five years in full-time evangelism. Yet faith causes us to move from God *can* to God *will*! Faith is a wonderful topic to preach about, but it is a wonder to experience!

I would like to offer wonderful words of counsel regarding faith, yet each time I attempt to do so, I realize I am not as far along as I should be. We have been taught that faith is a muscle, the more it is used the more it develops. Yet I find myself frequently relearning old lessons.

Before God called me to preach I had a comfortable position as a director of marketing. When I left this position to pastor, my salary dropped by two-thirds from one week to the next! Upon receiving my first "church check", I noted that hospitalization, retirement, and car allowance were part *of* the package and not in addition to the package! Then the treasurer took it upon himself to reduce the entire benefit package by 10 percent from the amount previously budgeted for the pastor. Yet Scripture says in *Philippians 4:19*

"But my God shall supply all your need according to his riches in glory by Christ Jesus."

God was able to take a difficult beginning and carry it through to a glorious conclusion.

After 15 years of what some would call a successful pastorate, I felt God's calling into full-time evangelism. My wife and I made plans to sell our custom home, reduce our standard of living by 50 percent, and move into my grandfather's one hundred-year-old farmhouse until we could build a new house. We had enough money in savings to meet Ron Blue's and Larry Burkett's approval. While our denomination, mission boards, seminaries, and colleges uphold the Biblical office of an evangelist, I soon found they did nothing to financially assist him! We had the privilege of seeing many saved. Yet much travel, too few meetings, and all savings depleted made for some difficult days.

After seeing God's blessing on *The Country Church*, a South Texas pastor asked me if I thought I was out of God's will during those five years in evangelism. I was able to share with him that five years of *living faith* in evangelism taught me more than 40 years of *learning about faith* ever did! (I was only able to share that after they pried my fingers off his throat!)

Once, in North Texas, we were invited by 10 churches to preach a two-week crusade. They would erect a large tent and we would make a concentrated attempt to evangelize that city. The churches would cover the expenses which included the tent, travel, etc. A box would be placed in the back for a love offering. Upon concluding a successful meeting, one of the pastors informed me that the churches had failed to underwrite the crusade and reluctantly they took all the expenses out of the love offering!

We left that town after two weeks with $300 less than our minimum living expenses! We headed from there to our next meeting outside Fort Worth, Texas. It was a good meeting in that 12 people were saved and others added to the church. This particulare church had a budgeted amount for revival with no travel expenses provided. So we headed home after three weeks with $475 less than it took to live on!

Arriving home, the first thing that caught my attention was a large tree which had blown over and crushed my cyclone fence! Later, while I was cutting away the tree, a cattleman I had once met drove up to the house. He had never been there before nor has he been there since. He said, "The Lord laid you and your wife on our hearts. We have just sold some cattle and would like to give you this little love offering." As he drove off, I looked at the check he had handed me in the amount of $480.

"But my God shall supply all your need according to his riches in glory by Christ Jesus." Philippians 4:19

Once in another state, I was leading a seminar on personal soul winning. A young pastor came up to me at the conclusion and commented, "An evangelist would never come to a church like mine." I asked him why not. He said, "We're a small church in Nogales, Arizona, and half of our offerings are in pesos. We are a very poor church, but strategically located between Mexico and the U.S.A."

My advice to him was to pray about the person God was leading him to have, invite him, and have the faith to trust God for the answer. I felt very good to be able to encourage this young man in his faith-walk until he said, "I have prayed, will you come?" At that moment I realized this chance meeting was not for him, but that it was orchestrated by God for me! He shared with me that his state evangelism department would pay my airfare, but $100 was the most the little church had ever taken up for a love offering. I told my wife, "Honey, I'll pack and you pray."

The meeting concluded with a good number being saved, twenty some odd if my memory serves me. In addition, the little church took up a love offering that when converted from pesos totaled $200!

When I arrived home, my wife showed me a letter that had come from a fourteen-year-old young lady whose father I had led to the Lord years earlier. Her grandmother had died leaving her a small amount of money. This young lady wanted to give us a love offering, and with the permission of her parent's, she sent a check for $400!

"But my God shall supply all your need according to his riches in glory by Christ Jesus." Philippians 4:19

In another instance, our car was wearing out and on its last legs. Try going to the bank and sharing with them that you are in evangelism, your income is derived from love offerings, and you would like a loan. "Don't call us, we'll call you!"

Soon after a pastor sells his pick-up, brings me the money, and says, "Use it to buy a car." Then a Christian in central Texas sells us his Chevy Cavalier with 31,000 miles on it for the same amount we received as a love gift from the pastor!

"But my God shall supply all your need according to his riches in glory by Christ Jesus." Philippians 4:19

Without these faith experiences it would have been far more difficult to see, that in the beginning, God created *The Country Church*. By faith, in late March, 1998, with seven saints, my wife and I saw God birth *The Country Church* of Guadalupe County. By faith, it began in our home, ironically on "Hard Luck Road". By faith, after growing to 37 people, we rented a former tavern which was now dedicated a tabernacle to our Lord. By faith, we trusted God for three acres of land now also dedicated a tabernacle to our Lord. By faith, we trusted God for another three acres of land on FM78 in Marion, Texas, needing $6,000 to make a down payment. We prayed and pulled out an old "milk can". God gave us $10,500 and paid the remaining $30,000 in six months.

By faith, on April 30, 2000, we dedicated an 11,000-square-foot building to the Lord for the purpose of winning and disciplining men and women, boys and girls for Christ. By faith, God led us to purchase an additional three acres in December, 2000. By faith, we trusted Him for an additional 23,000-square-foot building to hold 1,200 people in worship and additional educational space. We now have trusted Him for an additional 7,000-square-foot pavilion for multi-purpose events, and two more acres with a modular building to house our benevolence ministries. As of this writing, there are plans to extend the auditorium to add 600 additional seats. Other plans include purchasing additional land, erecting an education building, and constructing an indoor arena.

By faith, we have come to see that God's plan for The Country Church is far greater than ours and more church starts are imminent. Join us in realizeing,

"But my God shall supply all your need according to his riches in glory by Christ Jesus." Philippians 4:19.

Chapter 4

The Focus

Many churches fail for lack of focus - basically, a blurred vision as opposed to the clear, distinct, purpose of the church. Other obstacles can result from a copycat mentality in the church. We observe a sister church and seek to duplicate rather than depend on the Holy Spirit of God to authenticate.

Another hindrance is yielding to the temptation of becoming program oriented rather than people sensitive. Oftentimes we take early retirement. We retreat to a comfort zone, becoming keepers of the aquarium rather then fishers of men. Dr. Adrian Rodgers said, "Either we evangelize or we fossilize."

Possibly the movie *Field of Dreams* has added to a change in church focus. "If we build it, they will come." Church has moved from *"Ekklesia"*, the called out ones, to the building that houses the church. The emphasis has shifted from baptisteries to birdbaths, from spiritual atmosphere to stain-glassed atriums.

The Country Church has a four-fold mission. When we understand our purpose it allows all that we do to line up with our reason for being here. The first mission of *The Country Church* is to exalt our Savior. The Lord Jesus is to have first place in all that we do. All the praise, the honor, and the glory for what has, is, and will be done are to go to Him. As Believers, we want to be caught up in all that He is. *Philippians 3:7-10* reads,

> *"But what things were gain to me, those I counted loss for Christ. Yea doubtless, and I count all things but loss for the excellency of the knowledge of Christ Jesus my Lord; for who I have suffered the loss of all things, and do count them but dung, that I may win Christ. And be found in him, not having mine own righteousness, which is of the law, but that which is through the faith of Christ, the righteousness which is of God by faith: That I may know*

him, and the power of his resurrection and the fellowship of his sufferings,
being made conformable unto his death."

The second mission of *The Country Church* is to evangelize those outside of
Christ. While many have religion, it is God's desire that we have a personal relationship with his Son, the Lord Jesus. The attitude of our society is that we are all trying
to get to that pearly white city, we are merely taking different paths. This spirit of
universalism has crept into the modern church.

We, *The Country Church*, believe that Jesus Christ is the way, the truth and the
life and that one cannot have eternal life apart from Him. People need to know the
Gospel, which we preach. *Romans 10:9-13* reads,

"That if thou shalt confess with thy mouth the Lord Jesus, and shalt believe
in thine heart that God hath raised him from the dead, thou shalt be saved.
For with the heart man believeth unto righteousness; and with the mouth
confession is made unto salvation. For the scripture saith, whosoever
believeth on him shall not be ashamed. For there is no difference between
the Jews and the Greek: for the same Lord over all is rich unto all that call
upon him. For whosoever shall call upon the name of the Lord shall be
saved."

The message of the Old Testament was come and hear, the message of the New
Testament is to go and tell. The frustration of the church is when New Testament
Believers seek to live by Old Testament motives, methods, and message. A sales/
marketing background has had an influence in my life. Principles like, "He that
knocketh on doors, getteth business," and "Nothing happens until someone signs on
the dotted line." It sheds great light on Jesus' words in *Luke 16:8*

"...for the children of this world are in their generation wiser than the chil-
dren of light."

Sadly, we have been ineffective in our method, and derelict in our mission. We
have hidden our light under the basket of apathy and indifference. Jesus makes a
statement which both Matthew and Mark have recorded that brings conviction to our
hearts. He says, "Follow me and I will make you (or make you to become) fishers of
men." When I am not fishing, I am not following!

There is a wondrous account in Luke 5. Jesus instructs Simon to lower his nets.
Simon Peter said, "At thy word I'll do it." The results were a bountiful boatload of
fish, in fact, more than enough for one boat. They needed help with the harvest! In
the expanded Greek translation Jesus says, "You shall be catching men alive." "Catching men alive?" The church must decide if this is fact or just a fish story?

The third mission of *The Country Church* is to edify the Believers in Christ. It is
our desire to build up the body - to encourage in the Word, the work and the will of

our Lord. We pray *The Country Church* will be the family that prays together, stands together, and lifts each other up.

In some churches today, contention is recognized as a spiritual gift! We coddle contention, we cuddle contention, but we do not Biblically "mark" contention. In *John 13:34-35* we read Jesus' words

> *"A new commandment I give unto you, that ye love one another; as I have loved you, that ye also love one another. By this shall all men know that yea are my disciples, if ye have love one to another."*

Contention, strife, and divisions do not have a rightful place in the body of Christ. The church is "relieved" when contention is dealt with.

I have a delightful, old, red tomcat named Sugar-Ray. He was given to me as part of a revival love offering! If Sugar-Ray has his tail caught under the rocker, nothing I can do will please him - gifts of tuna, bowls of milk are all to no avail! In fact, he will "tear up" those who come near him! What is not needed is a gift nor a compromise but simply to get Sugar-Ray's tail out from under the rocker!

We have all heard the story of the man who fell asleep in the barber's chair. Two young boys smeared Limburger Cheese in his moustache. When he awoke, he paid the barber, and began to sniff the air. He moved around the shop, sniffing as he went. Out the door, nose up, sniffing and still the man lumbered down the block, around the block, and back to the barbershop again. He stuck his head in the door of the barbershop and said, "Fellows, I have news for you, the whole world stinks!" Could it be the church has allowed the "Limburger Lip" to rule and reign, and the mission and ministry of the church has been hindered by it?

The final mission of *The Country Church* is to equip the Believers to do the work of the Lord. In the new member's class, a lesson is taught on "Finding My Place in *The Country Church*". The lesson includes a study of ministry gifts and a spiritual gifts inventory.

He has saved us for service to Him. A fruitful, contented Christian is one who has found his spiritual gift(s) and is operating in them for Christ's glory. Before being enrolled in a Sunday Bible study class, each new member is encouraged to attend an eight-week course for new members taught by the pastor. This is held every eight weeks on a continuing basis (available upon request).

James writes under the inspiration of God's Holy Spirit that we are to *"Be doers of the Word and not hearers only."* Ours is to be a hands-on ministry with encouragement given to ministry, missions, and building projects. To the Church at Ephesus, Paul wrote,

> *"And he gave some apostles: and some prophets; and some, evangelists; and some, pastors and teachers; For the perfecting of the saints, for the work of the ministry, for the edifying of the body of Christ: Till we all come in the unity of the faith, and the knowledge of the Son of God, unto a perfect*

man, unto the measure of the stature of the fullness of Christ: That we hence-forth be no more children, tossed to and fro, and carried about with every wind of doctrine, by the sleight of men, and cunning craftiness, whereby they lie in wait to deceive; but speaking the truth in love, may grow up into him in all things, which is the head, even Christ. From whom the whole body fitly joined together and compacted by that which every joint supplieth, according to the effectual working in the measure of every part, maketh increase of the body unto the edifying of itself in love." Ephesians 4:11-16

Amen and amen!

Chapter 5

The Family

We sing a song entitled "The Family of God." It begins with, "I'm so glad I'm a part of the family of God, I've been washed in the fountain, cleansed by His blood…" At *The Country Church*, we are truly family. The word "family" has a warm, tingly, fuzzy feeling about it!

We use a term today, "dysfunctional family", to describe that family which is abnormal, impaired, or incomplete.

Some have used or abused that term to excuse every character flaw in their lives. I am "this way" because I was raised in a dysfunctional home. I think "this way" because of a dysfunctional upbringing. "The way I act is due to a dysfunctional home life." Have you had enough?

My mother died when I was six years old. Years later my Dad remarried. The woman he married continually made him choose between his wife and his children. We children were the victims of harsh and sometimes cruel punishment. At age 10, I got two shirts dirty in the same day. The punishment was that from age 10, until I left home at age 18, I was to do all my own washing and ironing.

A normal school day for me consisted of rising early, preparing my own clothes, fixing my own breakfast and lunch, and catching the bus on time. After-school activities consisted of cooking a cornmeal mush for the animals and cleaning pens for my stepmother's 20-plus registered dogs. I would then hand-feed and "slop" (only the truly "country" can appreciate this!) 100 head of hogs. Next it was time to bring up, pen and feed the cattle. At dark we moved inside, where it was my sister's responsibility to clean and prepare the evening meal. After supper, we boiled water, washed, dried, and put away every dish used that entire day. What studying was done happened just before flopping exhausted into bed, only to repeat this whole process on the morow.

Many people at *The Country Church* have had dysfunctional lives. In fact, it is almost a requirement! Some of our people come from broken homes. Some have married and divorced multiple times. One man at our church asked an engaged man if the pastor was doing his pre-marital counseling. The groom-to-be replied, "Yes, he is." This man responded, "What are you going to him for? He's only been married once. *I've* 'lost the farm' on three occasions."

Some come to the church living in fornication (although they didn't call it that!). Some come having abused drugs and alcohol. Yet scripture says,

> *"Therefore if any man be in Christ, he is a new creature: old things are passed away; behold, all things are become new." II Corinthians 5:17*

When a man, woman, boy or girl realizes he is lost, asks Christ's forgiveness and invites Him into his heart and life, that person is not only saved but a part of the family of God. No longer is he dysfunctional but complete in Him! Mark records an event in the life of Jesus in *Mark 3:31-35.*

> *"There came then his brethren and his mother, and standing without, sent unto him, calling him. And the multitude sat about him, and they said unto him, behold, thy mother and thy brethren without seek for thee. And he answered them, saying, who is my mother, or my brethren? And he looked round about on them which sat about him, and said, behold my mother and my brethren! For whatsoever shall do the will of God, the same is my brother, and my sister, and mother."*

Family! Many in the ministry have been taught to remove themselves from the people in the pew. Some desire the term "Doctor," others prefer the term "Reverend," or "The Reverend Doctor." Yet, I can think of no greater greeting than the one that begins with "brother" or "sister!" Family!

The Country Church was created in trust – trust in the pastor and the pastor trusting the people in the pew. It is absolutely necessary to have trust for *The Country Church* to function. We even have a group called "Trustees" in whom the work has been entrusted. This enables us to operate without the usual committee structure.

Having been a part of conventional churches for years, there are several things I've taken notice of. One, we can trust someone to take our children on a ski trip, but we cannot trust that person with the church's credit card. We have those to whom we trust for the care of our precious babies, but we cannot trust them to purchase nursery furniture without deacon approval!

When *The Country Church* was established, the precious deacons who were a part purposed to be identified by their service rather than by the board on which they served on. To this day *The Country Church* has no deacon board, yet it is blessed in having a higher percentage of deacons than many of our sister churches. Over the years I have been blessed by many deacon friends and have yet to share one deacon joke. They have been true servants of our Lord and to His church.

When our church was established, it was requested that the pastor hires and, if necessary, fires all staff. (This will be explained in greater depth in the chapters "The Finances", and "The Faculty.") In the wisdom and experience of the body, it did not seem fair that Scripture holds the pastor responsible for the oversight of the church, and then have the staff answer to a personnel committee.

Because *The Country Church* operates on percentage control as opposed to dollar control, staff is added as needed, subject to funds in the salary escrow. It has been our ministry philosophy to have the highest paid bi-vocational staff as opposed to the lowest paid full-time staff. This gives us maximum ministry in areas often neglected as the church struggles to call another full-time staff.

This does not mean the church does not have, nor will not consider, other full-time staff. It does mean that in this and other areas both stewardship and productivity are of the utmost importance. The staff at *The Country Church* are both friends and family. While each of us has distinctive gifts and responsibilities, we are able to yield to each other for the good of the body. Each staff member is to pray for and encourage the others in the work God has called them to do. Every attempt is made to eliminate competition and zones, and to foster feelings of family.

Mission churches, present and future, are part of *The Country Church* family. It would be a terrible thing to see a family bring offspring into the world and then neglect, abandon, or be jealous of them. It is our prayer that each church plant prospers above ourselves. In I, II and III John, the beloved apostle repeatedly writes to the children. Actually to the "elect lady and her children". His prayer is that they would "walk well", that they would prosper and be in health even as their souls were prospering.

Plans are for each mission church, a long with *The Country Church,* to pool resources so that in a cooperative, family atmosphere additional churches might be planted for the glory of God.

Chapter 6

The Fishing

Someone told the story of a man confronting his wife after she had spent the entire day shopping. "Honey, why is it that you say you've been shopping and yet you rarely buy anything?" She replied, "I don't know dear, why is it you say you are going fishing and you never catch anything?"

Another story is told of the game warden that had received a reliable tip that Fred had been "dynamiting" for fish. The game warden approached Fred's boat and seeing no fishing tackle said, "Fred, I don't see any tackle and you know it's against the law to dynamite for fish!" Fred calmly lit a sick of dynamite, handed it to the game warden and said, "Sir, do you want to sit here and talk or would you rather fish?"

It is not a question whether the church is to fish or not.

The only question open for debate is, How?

The Country Church tries to be faithful in fishing for the souls of men. We listen, we learn, we cast. We use different methods in our efforts to "catch men alive" for His glory in the church.

We want to share some of the "tackle," or the bait, that has been used in our fishing. We desire to see ourselves as commercial rather than recreational fishermen, for our lives and livelihood depend upon it! *The Country Church* tries to be visible in the market place. If we want to catch fish we must go to where the fish are.

When a business is seeking to attract customers, it first identifies those it is trying to reach. Then the business explores the most comprehensive and cost effective way to accomplish the tasks. For years, our church advertising consisted of Christian radio, the newspaper religion page, and the yellow pages under the heading "churches." These are wonderful ways to attract the Believers, but who said, "There is rejoicing in heaven over he who transfereth his letter?"

In order to reach our target audience, *The Country Church* advertises at two local cattle auctions. At one of the auctions there is a lighted *Country Church* sign positioned between "Dodge Trucks are Ram Tough" and "Acco Feeds for the Committed Cattleman". Our sign is simple and to the point:

The Country Church for Country Folks
1005 FM78, Marion, Texas
Phone number (830) 914-4749

In another auction barn hangs a 4-by-8 sign which reads:

The Country Church
1005 FM78, Marion, Texas
Phone number (830) 914-4749

"And the hand of the Lord was with them; and a great number believed, and turned unto the Lord." Acts 11:21

Both of these signs are in places where many unchurched are.

Our radio advertising is done periodically on two local radio stations. These two stations are in large communities ten miles from the church. We allow them to bid for our business. Both of the stations are of a secular country-western flavor. We may not agree with the music, but the method is to fish where the fish are. Our advertising approach consists of saturation advertising for approximately a month on a given station. By advertising extensively for a period of time and then stopping, we are able to assess its effectiveness by the number of visitors attending our church.

We have experimented with television advertising. Surprisingly, to create and shoot a 30-second ad cost only about $800. These ads can then be used on anything from public access television to "Movies For Guys Who Like Movies" on TNT. Again, where are the fish and how do we reach them?

Sometimes *The Country Church* uses big events to disarm the skeptic and raise the visibility of the church. For example, once a year we host a free country breakfast. We serve thick-sliced peppered bacon, pure pork sausage, *panas* (a German meat dish), and scrambled eggs, biscuits and gravy. Add to that orange juice and a bottomless cup of coffee. We enlist local Country and Southern Gospel singers who sing round robin while folks are eating breakfast. The pastor, staff, and church leaders are in a high profile, yet non-threatening environment as they "serve" the community.

Consider the message conveyed. One denominational church in town is selling plate lunches for $4.95 to raise money for their church. Another is selling egg tacos and holding yard sales to keep their church afloat. On the other hand, the message that comes forth from *The Country Church* is that God isn't destitute! Our people really care! If the partakers insist on paying for their meals, we tell them one visit to *The Country Church* is all it costs!

We have found most lost folks don't care about our revivals or high attendance days. Therefore, each year before our Bible Conference, we have a Saturday Night Country Gospel singing, and feed everyone who attends free 1/3 pound grain-fed hamburgers. For this event we cover the musician's stipend. After a good meal and great music the crowd is primed for Sunday morning's kickoff.

With each special event we rent portable signs from our volunteer fire department. These signs are placed on strategic arteries within ten miles of the church. The signs give us contact with a receptive audience in the fire department as well as in the community.

The Country Church is located between three cities with populations between 20,000 and 40,000. Each of these cities has a large regional grocery chain servicing its area. We have agreed to advertise on the back of their cash register receipts for ninety days. Due to their tremendous sales volume we can expect 648,000 hits in ninety days! If we were to connect with one-tenth of one percent of these people, this would equate to 648 visitors over a three-month period!

The Country Church is located in a town populated with approximately 1000 people. The phenomenon is that since its inception, *The Country Church* has averaged between forty and fifty first-time visitors each week for almost six years! Have we "caught" them all? No, but we'll keep fishing!

All of the aforementioned advertising or marketing plans are merely tools to secure prospects for one-on-one visitation. With all of the plans and programs in church life, nothing takes the place of Biblically going out two by two to reach a lost world for Christ.

Because *The Country Church* is short on committee meetings, we have the opportunity to be long on visitation. Consider this fact: the average evangelical church has one night per week set aside for visitation. Most of us have come to realize that visitation is not the largest attended event in the local church. If visits are missed, when, if ever, are the visitors contacted?

In our new members class we are seeking to address this issue. Over the years, I have become convinced that we have lost generations to the Biblical work of soul winning. We have Believers in our churches who are forty, fifty, sixty and seventy years of age who have never shared their faith with a lost person. For the sake of the kingdom and the salvation of souls we must reverse the trend! Hence the third lesson in the new members class is devoted to soul winning.

The good news is that each lost person who comes to Christ has another whole circle of influence. He invites his family and friends who in turn do the same.

While there are many training tools available for visitation, one simple tool that is easy to share is "F.O.R.M.A.L.ity." The first thing mentioned upon a visit to a person's home is *F*amily. We open the visit speaking of family and look for bridges to cross and a foundation to build on. The next subject is

*O*ccupation. This helps to bring them in contact with Christians in their career field. *R* is for religion. People feel comfortable discussing religion, but are oftentimes uncomfortable speaking about a relationship with Christ. Church background is a real door opener to present the claims of Christ. *M* is to make a presentation of the Gospel. We share our personal testimonies of how we came to a saving knowledge of Christ with supporting Scripture. *A* is to ask if this has ever happened to him. If not, ask if there is any reason why he wouldn't be willing to pray now in the privacy of his home to receive Christ. *L* is to leave the door open for another visit. The *ity* of the word "formality" is "*I*t *T*akes *Y*ou."

Someone once said, "If we catch fire, people will come to watch us burn!" This can have both a positive and a negative impact. If the church does not keep evangelism in the forefront, we will attract a group drawn to the popularity of the church who have not bought into the authority and mission of the church.

The County Church has sought to be a "light to the lost" rather than a "drawing to the dissatisfied." Since soul winning is our priority, 50 to 55 percent of the church membership has come by kingdom growth rather than by transfer growth. And, we have discovered that with evangelism being the priority, those who come just for a show don't stick around. The result is that *The Country Church* is filled with people who have been saved as a result of our fishing, and people who truly care about reaching the lost. They have become soul-winning disciples and active members. God bless and good fishing!

Chapter 7

The Finances

There are countless ways our Lord has blessed *The Country Church* concept, one of which is the finances. The pastor's secular background consisted of work in sales, sales management, marketing, budgets, balances, and forecasts. Needed and necessary, no doubt. Yet to what degree? At what cost? Over fifteen years in sales revealed a circle of events that all too frequently repeat themselves.

At my company we would strive to increase sales and profitability. When this goal was achieved, we then were able to hire more people to measure sales and profitability. The next step was to hand down more exhaustive and complex reports to be filled out by the sales force. The work purpose then shifted from sales to reporting. When sales began to drop, intense reporting was temporarily shelved and a re-emphasis on sales and profitability was reinstated by the company.

This futile circle of events was reoccurring, much like the children of Israel who walked with God, experienced God's blessing, sinned, experienced God's displeasure and correction, repented and again walked with God as the cycle continued.

Much of this same futility is replayed in church finances. For many of us, it has been difficult to break out of a fruitless cycle where the reporting and micro-managing of mammon has superceded the saving of souls.

How many times have we heard, "Is tonight a business meeting?" Is there one among us who didn't understand the question? In other words, "business meeting" was not taken to mean "blessed meeting" and so they saturated our services with their absence!

We, who attended, became more zealous. We implemented church suppers, in an all out effort to bait and switch! Let them come for "the beef" and hit them with "the business!" What followed then was we found our people were not that hungry. It was time for serious saints to take serious action! In one of those scheduled meet-

31

ings we voted to move the meeting time to Sunday nights. At last, a day and hour available to the masses! Surely they will pack our pews to hear our blessed moderator say, "We will now consider ourselves in a business meeting." If a tree falls in the forest and no one is there to hear, is there sound?

The last effort, with back against the wall, is to approach the pastor on this serious situation. "Pastor, would you preach a message entitled, "Why I'm a Premillennialist and Faithfully Attend Business Meetings"?

Most of us have endured the undesired and endless business meeting where the focus was on whether to spend $7.95 or $10.95 on a gallon of paint for the nursery. We have lived for years with the "two broom" mentality folk - those whose annual contributions went to buy two brooms, yet they fumed over every line item.

The question arose during the embryonic stages of *The Country Church,* is there a simple method or pattern to handle the financial affairs of the church? Will simplicity in finances work in a church setting? Looking back we can answer that question with a yes. Can a financial format be presented for everyone's perusal that does not require a Philadelphia lawyer with an MBA to interpret? Yes it can! Will it meet the need of every church? No, it will not!

At the end of this chapter you will find a simple financial worksheet and examples that we would like to comment on. One financial statement shows the beginning of this ministry, the other is the August, 2004 financial statement. Granted, it is far easier to implement a new work than to change an existing work.

From its inception, *The Country Church* has operated on a percentage-controlled budget. While the overall budget is percentage controlled, there are dollar-controlled line items. An example: the Southern Baptist Convention (SBC) may be in the mission budget for a percentage, while a local evangelist may be listed with a dollar amount.

When *The Country Church* adopted this procedure, one of the comments was, "It may work for a handful in a home, but it will fail to work with a houseful in a permanent building." Some six and a half years later, our financial plan continues to work with the simplistic focus for which it was intended.

As one examines the worksheet, he will notice that it is divided into four major categories that are percentage controlled. Much time could be spent discussing how many categories are needed, and the percentages should be directed by the Holy Spirit for each individual church. The following format will help to understand the reason, dialog, and prayer that led to *The Country Church's* financial plan.

First was the matter of missions. Many of us were of the school that if individuals tithed and brought to the Lord their first fruits, so also should the church return its first fruits. It was purposed early on that building, salaries, and other costs would not be funded at the expense of missions. We, as a church or a people, would not offer up to God "summer fruit."

Each church must seek its own understanding of what constitutes "missions." For some it is primarily evangelism and it's funding. For others, missions include Christian institutions of higher education or pastoral training. Still others include crisis pregnancy centers and various benevolent or social ministries as missions. Some mission receiving organizations/agencies cry for funding while supporting elaborate arbors, atriums, meditation lakes, and jogging trails while little is done for the advancement of the cause of Christ. Prayer, care and purpose must proceed the establishing of a Christ-honoring mission budget. Those receiving mission funding should also be encouraged to pray for those God is using as a source of their sustenance.

The second category is for building and maintenance, which is at 25 percent. While this may not be a Biblical percentage, it is one that even the most conservative financial institution would feel comfortable with. Since the beginning of *The Country Church*, we have not indebted ourselves outside this parameter. While it is always better to pay cash up front, there may be circumstances to hinder or prevent it. This is an area I would certainly yield to the financial freedom folks if I had some assurance that they began under similar circumstances.

The Country Church began in 1998 with nine people including the pastor and his wife. The first offering was $250, $150 of which was given by the pastor. Due to rapid conversion growth, the church moved from a home, to a vacant tavern, to a new 11,000-square-foot facility in less than two years. Constructive criticism came from a dear friend who was committed to zero indebtedness. However, his circumstances were entirely different. He pastored a mature congregation of 200-plus people. They were housed in a facility accommodating 600. And from a recent land sale, they had "x" number of dollars in the bank!

The third category could be listed as "all other" or "miscellaneous." This covers everything from envelopes to literature. This was a category that caused some concern; However, we have found it has adequately covered these expenses.

The fourth and final category is listed as salaries. Our percentage here is 55 percent. This percentage came from SBC financial information. When all SBC church salary percentages were averaged this is the way the percentage came forth. Some smaller churches had a slightly larger percentage, which enabled them to call their first full-time pastor.

When *The Country Church* was started, it was determined that the pastor would be responsible for the hiring, and if necessary, the firing of all staff. Our first staff person was our beloved praise and worship leader, Phil Jewett. As he and I shared our philosophies of ministry and financial structure, I asked what he would consider to be a fair stipend. He replied, "After 30 years in the ministry, no one has ever asked me that question!" He asked if we could work a 60/40 division much like our revival meetings. We agreed that we would begin here and later "cap" our salaries so additional staff might be brought on.

Our ministry philosophy is basically that we would rather have the highest paid bi-vocational staff as opposed to the poorest full-time staff. This has worked well for us even with considerable growth. We have found when one can make both a house and car payment on a bi-vocational salary, he is both content and productive. Also, little time is spent on a search for significance, or other ministry opportunities.

The finances have increased to the point where our mission church starts and salary supplements are also supplied through this category.

We would be derelict in failing to mention our receiving of the harvest. *The Country Church* does not operate by pledging the budget, choosing instead to teach Biblical stewardship, and then trust the Lord for the increase. There are no offering plates passed; however, a picnic basket is provided in the foyer for those who bring tithes and offerings to the Lord's house.

During our first year we had an opportunity to purchase three acres of land. We were some forty or fifty strong at the time and needed $6,000 to close. My wife had an antique milk can that we set in the middle of the Old Tavern floor. For four weeks we prayed. The fifth week we dropped our love offerings in the old milk can. The men counted the money and came up with $10,543 for which we praise the Lord! The old milk can is now a permanent part of our building program.

During revivals, Bible conferences, and the like, a "boot offering" is received. Two cowboy boots are placed by exit doors and generous love offerings are always the result. For *The Country Church,* simplicity can and does work as a great God continues to meet our needs.

Over the years, we have come to believe that there are several "chinks" in the traditional Church's financial armor. For instance, in most traditional congregations, the church encourages members to tithe, then asks them to buy Sunday School material, pay for refreshments, buy flowers, and hold a car wash and bake sale to pay for the kids to go to camp! The people frustratingly ask, "What is our tithe used for?" At *The Country Church*, we hope our members can clearly see the ways their tithes are being allocated.

Also, it is our belief that the Christian Church has done a commendable job teaching new Believers that, "The tithe is the Lord's." However, it appears we have failed in helping our people learn to live on the remaining 90 percent! As we strive to correct this problem, more money will become available for ministry and for reaching the world with the Gospel of Christ.

The Country Church

MARION, TEXAS

Receipts for March 1998	MISSIONS (10%)		BUILDING MAINT. (25%)		MISC. (10%)	SALARIES (55%)		BALANCE	
$2,516.00	251.	60	$629.00		$251.60	$1,383.80			$2,516.00
	SBC/SBT (5%)	$125.80	Lillian Reinhart Deposit	$300.00	Bible book store		Bro. Ikels	$830.28	
	Clifton Jansky	$50.00			Literature		Bro. Jewett	$553.52	
	Dennis Evin	$50.00			K-Mart				
					5 flower barrels				
TOTALS		$225.80		$300.00	$242.92	$1383.80		$2152.52	
BALANCE		$25.80		$329.00	$8.68	$0.00		$363.48	

35

The Country Church Financial Statement
For Month Ending August 31, 2004

Balance Forward:	450,037.93	Total Receipts Balance Forward:	581,060.93	Building Loan Balance: $639,200.05
Current Month Receipts:	100,969.22	Less Total Disbursement:	153,747.70	
Special Receipts:	30,053.78	Ending Balance	427,313.14	
Total Receipts Balance Forward:	581,060.93			

MISSIONS (10%)		Building Maintenance (25%)		Miscellaneous (10%)		Salaries (55%)	
Balance Forward:	2,986.03	Balance Forward:	272,496.37	Balance Forward:	19,081.74	Balance Forward:	155,473.79
Receipts	10,096.92	Receipts	25,242.31	Receipts	10,096.92	Receipts	55,533.07
Additional Gifts	3,830.95	Additional Gifts	16,170.87	Additional Gifts	2,192.96	Additional Gifts	7,859.00
Subtotal Giving	16,913.90	Subtotal Giving	313,909.54	Subtotal Giving	31,371.62	Subtotal Giving	218,865.87

MISSIONS		Building Maintenance		Miscellaneous		Salaries	
New Tribes Missions	100.00	Sound Equip./Power Point	394.58	Kitchen/Cleaning Supplies	915.91	Payroll	27,721.08
Vertical Ministries	50.00	G.V.E.C.	2,029.96	Refreshments	366.82	Traffic Control	200.00
R.B.C. Ministries	50.00	Green Valley Water	80.60	Office Expenses	1,876.19	Insurance	3,716.04
Marion International Minist.	50.00	Telephone	391.07	G.E. Capital Copier Lease	238.15	Gas Allowance	150.00
Gideons International	50.00	Avaya Telephone Lease	181.36	Literature	3,646.98	Jail Ministry/Gas	100.00
San Antonio Rescue Mission	50.00	Building Loan Payments	10,000.00	Children's Ministry	83.08	Staff Misc. Expenses	380.92
Cadence International	100.00	Waste Management	172.95	VBS	63.89	Sprint	998.30
Clifton Jansky	100.00	Security One	25.00	Youth Ministry	175.09	Ladies Retreat	78.25
Seguin Pregnancy Center	100.00	Helping Hand Hardware	439.81	Flowers	19.18	Bro. A. Shepherd Honorarium	300.00
Guad. Co. Detention Ministry	100.00	Church Mutual Insurance	929.00	Nursery	246.69	Wild Horse Ministry	12,263.19
Dennis Erwin	100.00	High Sierra Toilet	89.50	Caps for Resale	696.00	Staff Retreat Deposit	100.00
David West	100.00	Materials & Supplies Etc.	1,005.61	Church Newsletter	396.94	Criswell College Tuition*	3,085.00
Criswell College	150.00	Lawn Maintenance	250.00			Covington Theo. Seminary	1,736.00
Bluebonnet Baptist Assoc.	250.00	Children's Bldg. Construction	59,762.27			Dr. A Street Travel Expense	200.00
RACAP	200.00	Pavilion Supplies, Etc.	596.03				
Calvary Commission	50.00	Nat'l Church Purch./Tables	431.00				
East TX Family Baptist Min.	100.00	Muzicom Internet	49.99				
Wild Horse Ministry	1,200.00	Countryside Const./Sewer	137.89				
SBC/SBT	5,036.57	Buzz Fence Co.*	4,450.00				
Mission Starts	1,007.31						
CC Attic (including utilities)	292.13						
CC Attic love offering	2,850.00						
Benevolence	412.51						
Jail Ministry Baptism Tub*	78.95						
Total Expenses	12,577.47	Total Expenses	81,416.62	Total Expenses	8,724.92	Total Expenses	51,028.78
Balance	4,336.43	Balance	232,492.92	Balance	22,646.70	Balance	167,837.09
*Covered with love offering.		*Covered with love offering.				*Partially covered with love offering.	

Chapter 8

The Facets

Many are the facets of *The Country Church* that have assisted us in reaching one more soul. We will share some of the methods used in our ministry with prayer they will inspire and reaffirm what you are already doing.

The first home of *The Country Church* was the living room of the Ikels' home on Hard Luck Road, outside Marion, Texas. Our next move brought us to a vacant building formerly used as a tavern. A "sanctified" bar, if there is such a thing, became our pulpit. The beer cooler was used for storage. The pool room became the ladies Sunday school class, the bottle room served the youth, while the nursery was taken from the dining area. The "real man's" Bible study met on the bar's dance floor!

As the Lord began to build His church, space became a premium. The only larger building in town, a dance hall, was leased to an antique mall before we knew it was available. Someone said, "Necessity is the mother of invention." So, some of the brethren hooked up a camcorder to a VCR in both the pool room and the bottle room in order to broadcast the service throughout the building. This gave us an increased seating capacity of 65.

Due to the success of this simple project, the idea was carried over into our first new building. Each of the perimeter classrooms had a cable hook-up and an inexpensive television monitor. Each classroom was totally equipped for less than $200! This allowed overflow crowds of 690-plus in an auditorium designed for 450.

How else could a church provide this much extra seating capacity for only $1,200? We decided to incorporate this feature in all additional buildings. When it comes to technical innovation, the author offers limited input due to his conviction that "if it has a plug *on it*, it has a demon *inside it!*"

In the foyer of *The Country Church* is a television monitor that serves several purposes. On screen is a welcome to guests as they enter along with a schedule of upcoming events. New member's pictures are also flashed across the screen, thanking the Lord for those He has sent our way! Again, an economical computer and a $200 television monitor make it all possible. Having a son with a computer science degree to boot doesn't hurt, but he does not come with a monitor. An additional charge is required!

We are blessed in that one of our charter members purchased a printing franchise in nearby San Antonio. They have used what God has given them to, in turn, minister unto the Lord. John wrote in his third epistle words that speak to each of us: *"Beloved, I wish above all things that thou mayest prosper and be in health, even as they soul prospereth." III John 1:2*

One of their printing capabilities is the ability to professionally produce directories from our digital camera. Each week new members are photographed with the digital camera. Once a month their photos are compiled, and these new additions are printed in alphabetical order. These are added to our existing directory so that we enjoy a church directory that is always up to date! The digital camera is also used each month in baptismal services. Each convert receives a picture to accompany his baptismal certificate.

Other inexpensive, yet valuable ministry tools include a dedicated power line for the sound system, and FM radios and earphones tied into the sound system for the hearing impaired, nursery pager, etc.

Another proven tool is the Internet. The church's website is listed as www.thecountrychurch.com. Our website provides the ability to listen to each Sunday's message and receive God's plan of salvation. It also provides a mapquest.com map for directions, contact information, and email capabilities. I can be written to at butch@thecountrychurch.com. My email goes to my secretary who in turn provides me with the information. We use this email address for important church business so no more Internet stories please!

Seems to me that too many pastors are spending too much time in front of a computer rather than before an open Bible. I have heard all the arguments, yet I prefer to sit with an open Bible on my lap - Kenneth S. Wuest's expanded Greek Translation on one side and a Strong's Exhaustive Concordance on the other!

Services follow a unique pattern that was birthed out of necessity. *The Country Church* started with nine members assembling on Sunday mornings. The pastor then held revival, Bible conferences and meetings on Sunday nights through Wednesday nights. Because of this, when we began Thursdays were set aside for midweek services and Saturday was designated for visitation.

The ladies soon requested a Tuesday night Bible study and complimented it with a Wednesday morning Bible study. This was followed by a Thursday morning prayer meeting where all weekly prayer requests were laid before the Lord. The men used Tuesday evenings and Saturday mornings for Bible study and workdays for building and improving the facilities. As time has passed, and because we do not have committee meetings, we now have the privilege of having visitation three days a week. In many evangelical churches, visitation nights have been replaced by "meeting" nights while the church wonders why the world is going to hell in a hand basket!

The Country Church attempts to stay focused on our mission. Again, we seek to evangelize the lost, exalt the Savior, edify the Believers, and equip the saints. Every action or involvement is prefaced by, "Where does it fit within our mission statement?"

Time will not permit, nor does space allow, adequate praise for our Country Church staff. Only eternity will bear out their contributions to Christ's kingdom.

Brother Phil Jewett leads us in praise and worship and works with "The Country Treasures," our senior adults. Additionally, he coordinates workdays, schedules events, and is an all-around servant of the Lord.

Praise and worship is possibly one of the most difficult responsibilities in the New Testament Church. For example, if someone did not like my preaching, chances are good that they would move on down the road. If someone does not like the music portion, however, I have found they will stay and complain about it!

Hymns? Hymn books? Praise music? Scripture songs? Surely we couldn't be against that! Contemporary, Country Gospel? Black Spirituals? High Church? Low Church? To "organ" or not "organ," that it is the question! Keyboards? Guitars? Banjos? Harmonicas? How about a flute? Yet through the fog, week after week we are led into heaven's throne room with an unbelievable balance of musical diversity.

The Country Treasures, our senior adults, are a blessing to behold. Far too many church growth experts (an expert is someone ordinarily out of town) have omitted the "graying of America" as possible target audiences. We have concerned ourselves with infants, tots, children, teens, boomer's, X'ers, and "blasters;" but by and large, we have neglected those who have paid the bills.

Years ago I attended a Bible conference and recorded the facts listed below. Dr. Wilbur Chapman once made a report where 4,500 people were present. Here is what he found:

- 19 out of 20 people who become Christians do so before they reach the age of 25.
- After 25 years of age, only one in 10,000 comes to know the Lord.
- After 35 years of age, only one in 50,000 comes to know the Lord.
- After 45 only one in 200,000 comes to know the Lord.
- After 55 only one in 300,000 comes to know the Lord.
- After 65 only one in 500,000 comes to know the Lord.
- After 75 only one in 700,000 comes to know the Lord.

"Youth must be won!"

For years I lived under the misconception that lost seniors could not be reached for Christ! In essence I have said, "If they are over 65 let them go to hell, we cannot reach them!" I have since learned not to let statistics circumvent the Holy Spirit of God. *The Country Church* has been blessed with a host of converts above the age of 50. Following are several relevant examples I would like to share with you.

Lucille S. was 87 years young. She was the matriarch of a large extended family we had led to the Lord. Everyone was praying for "grandma" and her salvation. Lucille heard the Word, the Gospel of her salvation. She believed on and received the lovely Lord Jesus. Her first words after her conversion were, "How can you baptize me and when?"

Lucille was baptized by immersion while seated in a chair held by a family member and myself. Was it real to her? The next week I received a beautiful card, a Bible marker, and two jars of homemade jelly from her! The card said, "Thank you so very much for leading me to the Lord and baptizing me."

Another such incident involved a man named Harry B. He was 85 years of age and lived in Seguin, Texas. He was the uncle of a childhood friend of mine. Harry informed me that he was dying of kidney failure and asked me to preach his funeral upon his death. I asked him my favorite question, "If you died tonight, do you know without a shadow of a doubt that you would be with Jesus?" Harry said, "No, I don't but I would like to." At 85 Harry received Christ as his personal savior. Now Harry knows even as also he is known.

Herbert S. was an 85 year-old professing atheist. He was somewhat of a recluse and was considered to be one of the most "frugal" individuals in Guadalupe County. Mr. S. insisted on selling his farm to either myself or my son while he retained the right to live on the property until his death. Seeing how I was then in full time evangelism and my son was a computer scientist, you can guess who bought the property!

After three years of refusing our feeble attempts to lead him to Christ, Mr. S. became ill and was forced to move to Seguin, Texas to live with his daughter. One Saturday, my son Keith and I paid a visit to Mr. S to attempt one final presentation of the Gospel. It was predetermined that Keith would visit with the daughter while I visited with the father.

The conversation began with him telling me, "Butch, I can't die! I want to, I try to, but I can't! I have even asked my daughter to find a doctor who would put me to sleep like a dog." I shared with him that the Lord wouldn't let him die. "Really, why not?" he asked. I said that if he died without Christ, he would split hell wide open. He listened to God's simple plan of salvation, and without prompting he closed his eyes, folded his hands, and out loud said, "Jesus, I'm a sinner. Would you forgive me of my sin, and save me? Amen." As we left, Mr. S. turned to my son and said, "Keith, I want you to have that 500 gallons of gasoline in my tank."

Was it real? Was there a change? Most certainly! The next week Mr. S. passed away. His daughter's words to my daughter–in-law were, "Daddy had the best day of his life after Butch and Keith's visit. The following day he slipped into a coma from which he did not awake." (I must add that he didn't awake from here.)

Our minister of education is Brother Mark Stough. This is a bi-vocational position, as Mark has a degree in Environmental Engineering and a master's in Christian Education. In addition to finding teaching material that best reflects *The Country Church*'s focus, he is charged with the training of teachers and oversees our visitation outreach.

This probably should not be in print, but when I first saw Mark's wife I instantly fell in love with her from which I have yet to recover. My wife Joan is very understanding of my plight because Mark married our only daughter! Mark's only comment has been, "I should have been more cautious about marrying a girl whose father called her 'the little princess!' "

Early on our youth were in the capable hands of David Kirkwood. Every week, day in and day out, David would lead one to three young people to Christ. Even at 40 years old he had the zeal and energy of a 20 year old. David has since been called to serve another congregation.

God has now provided us with Shane Osborn, a young man with a burden for discipleship of our youth. Shane loves the Lord and our young people. We are so blessed to have him serving with us. His address is unavailable, and should a church dare to call him, we will advise them how cheap "hit men" are to employ in Guadalupe County, Texas!

Children's ministries began under the very capable hands of Joan Ikels, the author's wife. After going through all submitted resumes, and considering countless concepts of what would people think, we allowed the Lord to do His work. Joan, in my opinion, is the queen mother of the forgotten ministry Vacation Bible School. She has organized and implemented a structure that has brought in over 650 children with upwards of 65 professions of faith in rural settings. During and after the invitation each church service, Joan counsels those children who have responded to an invitation during services or in Children's Church. Her ministry began many years ago when she led our own children to faith in Christ. Our daughter, Melissa now serves in this capacity.

For two years, *The Country Church's* office was in the very capable hands of Lois Payton. Lois once was the pastor's secretary for a large San Antonio megachurch. While visiting another church's office, a friend of hers told me Lois had recently retired, yet, was becoming restless and bored. On the spot, I called and told her that God wanted to bless her with the best boss she had ever had! (Evidently she had heard that line before, for she felt like she knew who that might be.)

Over the phone I shared with Lois how *The Country Church* wanted someone to come in late, leave early, spend two hours a day in Wal-Mart shopping for grandchildren, and be willing to work for $50 an hour. The secretary of the church I was calling from said, "Tell her this is a business phone, please hang up and I'll take the job!"

Seriously though, Lois did accept the position of church secretary. Due to her experience, this dear lady could handle more work in 20 hours than many younger could in 40! Many churches lose by providing a job profile and neglecting the Holy Spirit's leading. Lois is now retired again and we have since hired two full-time secretaries due to an ever-increasing membership Sharon Bauwens and Norma Lane. Sharon and Norma are invaluable members of our ministry team. We will do most anything to keep them including hiring the previously mentioned hit men.

Next on our bi-vocational staff is the Women's Ministry Director Ruth Ann Jewett.

Ruth Ann does an outstanding job of working with the ladies of our church. She leads out in Women's Bible studies and counseling of our church's women. She is also a gifted piano player!

The Country Church began with a retired person serving the Lord through a hospital, nursing home, and shut-ins ministry. What a valuable service our dear "Brother Bill" rendered to the Lord and this church. This ministry is now held by Dennis Johnson who, with his wife Winnie, makes the first hospital contacts. Dennis combines this job with our church's ever growing counseling ministry.

While as pastor, I wear many hats, none has been more rewarding than teaching the New Members class. I personally wrote the curriculum to meet the basic needs of the new convert or new member. This eight-week study bonds, blesses, and benefits both the pastor and the student. The lessons include The Inward Possession, The Outward Profession, Sharing Your Faith, The Local Church in God's Plan, How to Study the Word of God, Christ's Return for His Bride, and Finding My Place in *The Country Church* (a study of ministry gifts, including a spiritual gifts inventory).

"For as the body is one, and hath many members, and all the members of that one body, being many, are one body: so also is Christ. For by one Spirit are we all baptized into one body, whether we be Jews or Gentiles, whether we be bond or free; and have been all made to drink into one Spirit. For the body is not one member, but many. 1 Corinthians 12:12-14

We have added an additional Phase II, New Members Class taught by our associate pastor and minister of outreach. This class was necessary to assimilate new converts into the mainstream Sunday school program. Many of our converts came out of denominations where membership was preceded by a religious course. After completion of the course, all further need for study was negated. Our phase II class has assisted these new converts in seeing the continual need for a Bible study program.

Chapter 9

The Festivities

When we deal with festivities in a church setting, our thoughts run from one extreme to the other. Is the foremost question ministry or manipulation? Is this an effort to give out or receive from? Will it be a blessing or a burden? What type of message will this send to the community? Is our motive to profit or to be profitable?

Case in point, in our community one church chooses to sell egg tacos to raise money for the church. Another sells plate lunches to build up the budget. Another has an annual carnival, raffle, and auction to secure funds for the Savior. What is the message beneath the merriment? That Jesus is destitute, His church is bankrupt, and the kingdom is in danger of collapsing.

The Country Church, from its inception, had a desire to put back into the community rather than receive from it; to elevate Christ's church from high-level begging to a channel from which the blessings of God might flow.

One such means of community stewardship is our annual Saturday morning free country breakfast. The menu consists of the finest, freshest ingredients possible. (After all, it is done in Jesus name!) Meat includes pan sausage, thick-sliced peppered bacon, and *panas* (a German meat dish). Scrambled eggs, biscuits, gravy, jelly, and picante sauce are also on the menu. All of this is topped off with orange juice and a bottomless cup of coffee.

The cost to the community is free! When people ask where to pay, our reply is that this meal is our way of saying, "The Lord loves you and so do we." If they insist, we say, "Your visiting us in one of our services would be pay-a-plenty!"

All menu items are purchased from local merchants rather than from the "mega-mart." This, too, is a means of ministering to the people we are trying to reach. It starts people talking and raises the visibility of the church in the community.

During the come–and–go breakfast, several local gospel groups are singing in a round robin fashion. The pastor, staff, and people of *The Country Church* are identified with name tags and are found serving. What a way to meet prospects - while carrying coffee and juice to provide refills.

The décor is country and conveys a friendly atmosphere. Real effort is made to advance Christianity rather then express "Churchianity." Many curiosity seekers have become Christians because they saw, rather then heard that Believers cared.

Another community event is held prior to a Saturday night Sunday morning evangelistic rally. This is advertised as a free country supper and free gospel music concert. It features grain-fed chicken fried steaks (a Texas favorite), 1/3-pound hamburgers and 1/2-pound BBQ chicken with all the fixings. The meat is donated by cattlemen in the church who see it as a means to win people to Christ.

The music concert is led by a local country gospel singer who has been saved, sanctified, and has turned from taverns to tabernacles. He now encourages other churches to incorporate these rallies into their evangelistic efforts.

Sunday morning music is provided by the same music evangelist with the pastor preaching. No love offering is taken with the church giving a generous sum from the general fund. Our last event of this sort resulted in 27 additions to the church.

All special events are advertised by every means possible - one of which is portable signs placed in four directions from the church six to ten miles out. These are rented from the local fire department which again raises the visibility of the church in the community.

Few Christians would consider Vacation Bible School a festivity. Yet, if it is properly prepared and prayed over, it will produce amazing results. For many dead and dying churches, V.B.S. has been reduced to a maintenance ministry. In some churches, the attitude is we want only our kids, at an opportune time, for us, with as little effort as possible. In almost 25 years of ministry, I have yet to see commencement night meet or exceed attendance on Easter Sunday morning.

Our fall festival in October is another opportunity to reach children. Petting zoos, pony rides, booths and games offer more touch points with the community. Children will come and hear under these conditions who would not have come otherwise.

About one year ago, several of our members asked to use the church on Friday nights for guitar practice. The result has the formation of the Country Family Band. It's been a blessing to see a completed Jew on the keyboard and hear a converted Mormon sing a song he has written entitled *"The Country Church,"* which he describes his coming to Christ.

This group has now become a once-a-month addition to our music program, special event music for our mission churches and to other congregations.

Soon to be presented will be Country Church booths at the two local county fairs. This will open up new and exciting opportunities to reach people for Christ. This year we will also host our first "Country Church Trail Ride." This event will begin on a Saturday and conclude at *The Country Church* on Sunday morning in time for services.

Another outreach involved *The Country Church* securing our county fairgrounds arena in order to bring in "Wild Horse Ministries." A wild horse from our area was "gentle-broke" in less than two hours while the gospel was shared!

Accompanying this event, free 1/3 pound grain fed hamburgers, homemade french fries, and soft drinks were offered. Again, determining your target audience allows a church to be both sensitive and creative in seeking to win souls.

This event has now evolved into a three-week tour in surrounding Texas towns within a 100-mile radius. It is amazing to see how far people will drive to church when a church will drive great distances to minister to them.

During these early years of ministry, every effort has been made to use special events to reach the lost. However, we realize "to whom much has been given, much is required." This year will be our first attempt to give back to the *Christian* community in the form of a regional, blow the doors off Bible conference.

The Country Church will host this conference in our new auditorium and make it available to small south Texas churches who may find it difficult to take groups to the metroplex.

When planning special events several things must be taken into consideration. In marketing we are taught not to advertise our weakness. The competition will do that for you! In the church our best foot should always be forward. If we plan a major event, we pull out all stops and seek to do our best for the master.

Try to avoid copy-cat Christianity in which someone will lead and others will follow. Trust in God's Holy Spirit for new ministry in new directions to reach new people.

Find a need and fill it! This is but a methodology that springs from a theology that people are lost without Christ and we must reach them. Dare to reach out!

The question arises, are there any downsides to these types of activities? Any opposition? The answer is yes! Yet it does not come from the outside but from the inside. The W.W.C.D.I. is at work in every church. You are aware of the group, *Won't Work, Can't Do It!* We lost several families in the beginning who could not stand to see God's money given away like that.

The Beloved John wrote,

> *"They went out from us, but they were not of us; for if they had been of us, they would no doubt have continued with us: but they went out, that they might be made manifest that they were not all of us." I John 2:19*

How can this situation be avoided or overcome? Only by consistent teaching of the joy of giving, and the worth of a soul. Outside of seeing a soul come to Christ, few things are as rewarding to a pastor as seeing the church *give* out of a heart that is in love with Jesus!

When we see this take place we stand in the shoes of the Apostle Paul. We see through his eyes and hear these words,

"More over, brethren, we do you to wit of the grace of God bestowed on the churches of Macedonia; How that in a great trial of affliction the abundance of their joy and their deep poverty abounded unto the riches of their liberality. For to their power, I bear record, yea, and beyond their power they were willing of themselves; Praying us with much entreaty that we would receive the gift, and take upon us the fellowship of the ministering to the saints. An this they did, not as we hoped, but first gave their own selves to the Lord, and unto us by the will of God. Insomuch that we desired Titus, that as he had begun, so he would also finish in you the same grace also. Therefore, as ye abound in everything, in faith, and utterance, and knowledge, and in all diligence, and in your love to us, see that ye abound in this grace also. I speak not by commandment, but by occasion of the forwardness of others, and to prove the sincerity of your love. For ye know the grace of our Lord Jesus Christ, that, though he was rich, yet for your sakes he became poor, that ye through His poverty might be rich." II Corinthians 8:1-9

It is clear that our giving is not to be based on our circumstance. These Corinthian Believers first gave of themselves. Giving brings Believers to maturity. Giving is a grace that we are instructed to grow in. It proves the sincerity of our love. For my sake, Jesus who was rich gave up His life. It blesses and benefits the people to learn these spiritual truths.

When our people see the results of giving to the community, it fosters a desire to do more and accomplish more in using great event's to reach the lost for Christ. In whatever manner the Lord leads, the church must get out from the security of its walls and dare to reach our world for Christ!

Chapter 10

The Facilities

The Country Church has had four changes of facilities. The first facility was located at the pastor's home on Hard Luck Road, Marion Texas. With a mother-in-law's apartment for the nursery and toddlers room, a two-car garage for a fellowship hall and Sunday school space, bedrooms for classrooms, and the living room for our worship center, we were set to go!

This arrangement lasted for about two months, until Easter Sunday found us on the lawn with preaching from the porch! The dogs and cat enjoyed the extra attention but the wife suggested that a move was in order. Thirty-nine people in our home on Easter Sunday.

Marion, Texas, is anyone's definition of a small town. It does not have a stop-light; however, it boasts of several stop signs! A dear friend of mine, a college professor, described it as a place churches would come to die. The town is home, however, to a 3-A school district which helps to understand the size of the rural draw.

To downtown Marion we went in search of a new facility. Outside of an empty grain bin, the only building available was a vacant tavern with wooden floors. One of the interesting things about a tavern is the lack of light. Two fifteen-watt light bulbs furnished the majority of the lighting for the entire building. One was a regular white bulb located over the cash register; the other was a nice shade of blue, located over the dance floor. The most adequate lighting in the whole place was in the pool room. (You can't shoot pool in the dark!)

Taking "the church" to see our new facilities was an interesting experience. As I showed them around, one of our couples began to weep softly. Having the great discernment and compassion that I do, I sensed they were overwhelmed with what God had provided. I placed my arms around them and shared, "Isn't God good?" The soft weeping turned to loud unintelligible wailing! Waiting for the sobs to subside, I asked them to share with me what was on their hearts. They replied, "None of our friends would come to this despicable, horrible, place. It's filthy!" (They hadn't seen the grain bin!)

I suggested they either get a new set of friends or wait until God gave us a "new building" before inviting them. They chose to move on down the road.

Armed with paint, Windex, Formula 409, brushes and brooms, our army charged the enemy's stronghold! The building was painted green and white to match the town's school colors. (We needed all the help we could get!) With 40 metal chairs and a karaoke sound system we were ready to do church! Granted some of the senior saints had reservations about the beer cooler!

Still other minor concerns were the bar, holes in the floor, and limited restroom facilities. All of these obstacles were overcome, however, by the excitement of knowing God was at work! With a barn wood sign and a wrought iron cowboy kneeling at the cross, *The Country Church* was opened for business in downtown Marion!

As time progressed, two small camper trailers were added for additional Sunday school classes and a growing number of patrons, or "pilgrims," as the case may be.

The growing number of seekers led one prominent citizen to share with the pastor, "The reason you are growing is that the same old Saturday night drunks stumble in thinking the bar's now open Sundays! The town was amazed as they saw what God could do with a bunch of old drunks who found Jesus!

As God continued to bless and souls were being saved, a dear pastor friend, Alexander Shepherd of Savannah Baptist Church, offered us the use of his church's baptistery. Oh the sight of *The Country Church* walking those three blocks for baptismal services!

Brother Shepherd is a dear black preacher friend who, while approaching 80 years of age, has "stayed by the stuff!" (That is South Texas talk for "committed to the Word of God!") *The Country Church* family wanted to find some way to show our appreciation to Brother Shephard and his church. The result was our providing the supplies and labor for the painting of their church. This dear pastor said with tears in his eyes, "You folks don't even have a church and here you are painting ours." Brother Shepherd and I agree that "race relations" isn't a sermon on Sunday morning, nor is exchanging pulpits, it's a way of life.

Our next plan was to purchase three acres of land on Farm Road 78 (3/10 of a mile west of Marion). After the land was paid for, continuing growth coupled with the unavailability of larger facilities propelled us forward in building plans.

Launching a building program with the majority of our people being new converts was exhilarating to say the least! Outside the church, one comment was, "That preacher built that new building himself and didn't even have a building committee!" The truth is we had the largest building committee in church history! Each of our members was encouraged to put down on a slip of paper his thought(s) for a new building. Some comments were as follows:
- build it as economically as possible; simple
- country flavor

- adequate restrooms
- single story (seniors wouldn't see the 2nd floor!)
- not to exceed our building receipts (See Finances)
- contract the building ourselves
- chairs rather than pews
- multi-purpose facility

When this list of requirements was compiled we moved ahead with absolutely no contention or strife. The freshness of new converts was a blessing to those of us who had been "rode hard and put away wet." They realized *we the Believers,* were the church of God, not the building. The building of God and this structure merely housed the church.

As we proceeded, God's miracle at Marion began to unfold. Our local bank, who in 100 years of operation had not made a long-term construction loan, agreed to lend what our love gifts did not cover.

Plans were changed during construction to eliminate hallways and use moveable partitions for two classrooms, thus enlarging church seating capacity. TV monitors were placed in four back classrooms to accommodate overflow. When all was said and done, we had constructed, furnished, and laid one acre of paved parking for less then $300,000. This 11,000-square-foot building would be our home for the next two years.

During construction we erected a 4' x 16' wooden sign. It read, "Temporary Home of *The Country Church*." Repeatedly people would ask, "Why does the sign read temporary? Wasn't the old bar your temporary home? One by one we had opportunity to share that this world was not our "home," we're just passing through!

The most exciting event to take place during the construction of the building was the building of the church. Sounds like a play on words doesn't it? We were continually reminded that Believers made up the church and the building doesn't!

One such example of this truth was a man named T.S. His wife was a Believer who God drew to *The "Tavern" Country Church* by the use of the sign of the old cowboy kneeling at the cross. That sign, plus a preacher in boots and jeans, gave her hope that her husband would attend a church like this. Her husband had been in enough bars during the week that coming to a "converted" one on Sunday wouldn't stretch him too much!

After a Sunday or two, T.S. showed up at the new building for men's work night. He said, "Preacher, I'm fairly good with tools and I'd like to help." While we were at the building, T.S. was asked where he was at with Jesus. The real church was added unto that night as one more was added to the kingdom.

The people of *The Country Church* prayed that souls would be saved of those whom God sent to help construct the building. Two such individuals were "sheet rockers." During a work break they asked, "are there any people like "us" in your services?"

They were told, "I'm not sure. What kind of people are you?" They referred to their skin color and surnames. The conversation turned to the color God was looking for. It wasn't white, black, brown, or yellow. It was red - those who were covered by the blood of Jesus! The result two more saved, sealed, sanctified, "sheet rockers" added to the kingdom!

When subcontractors submitted their bids, we informed them we only wrote checks on Sunday mornings. It's amazing what that one little procedure will do for attendance!

During the two years in the new building, it was obvious that each time we tried to determine our circle of influence, God enlarged our circle! Just as there are problems in declining or plateau churches, there are also problems in growing churches.

In *The Country Church* where "folksy, fellowship, and friendly" are adjectives to describe our body, fear arose! What if we get too big? What if we lose what we have here?

At this time we had already sponsored three mission churches that were doing well, yet God continued to add to us numerically. One sweet, little lady said, "Preacher, how about running a few off so I can find a place to park?"

This was a time

"to be still and know that I am God..." Psalm 46:10.

A time to reconsider *Psalm 127:1:*

"Except the Lord build the house, they labour in vain that build it: except the Lord keep the city, the watchman waketh but in vain."

We began to share with the people God had sent us. He was ever widening our circle of responsibility. Someone asked, "How big do we want to grow?" Our growth was already far greater than any vision we might have had. It boiled down to two alternates: one, we could step out in faith and provide for those God was sending our way, or two, we could at least have the integrity to place a sign on the highway which read, "Go to hell, our church is full!"

Praise the Lord, *The Country Church* went with option number one! And, we needed God to work another miracle, or as it were miracles.

In miracle number one, God softened the heart of the adjacent landowner who agreed to sell us an additional three acres. Miracle number two involved getting the pastor's heart right. (It always has to come to that!) How would we raise the money for the land? Who would God use? God began to speak during my study time. What about you Pastor?

Okay, Lord, I've got an upcoming revival meeting, and if they are generous with a love offering, so shall your servant be. This didn't seem to impress the Lord and He spoke in terms of giving it all! In fact, it went something like this, "You have three revivals scheduled for the fall; why not give it all to me to multiply?" Then and only then, can you expect the people to give sacrificially. Long story made short, I did, they did, and God gave us three additional acres!

What to build? How big? Easy - big enough to house those God would send us and small enough so we didn't look like a "BB" in a boxcar. Sounds relatively simple doesn't it?

At a former church, I had asked Dr. Paige Patterson what he thought of a certain size auditorium in a rural, open-air setting. His reply, "If you plan on planting your life there, it may not be big enough; if not, it is too big, not everyone gets excited about driving down back roads."

Dr. Alan Streett, Professor of Evangelism at Criswell College, said, "Butch, as God gives you direction in sharing the miracle at Marion, please make mention that the town has no traffic light!" If it did, we would never get anything done, just watching it change colors and all!

The late Dr. W.A. Criswell influenced my life in many ways. One of his statements seemed to stick with me. Dr. Criswell said, "I would rather live on a flagpole in downtown Dallas than on the largest ranch in South Texas." I remember thinking, "Thank you Lord, for one less city slicker moving to the country!"

With fear and trembling we completed our plans for a 22,000-plus square-foot building. This would seat 1,100 for worship. There are certainly larger auditoriums; however, few of them are in towns with a population of 1,099! *The Country Church* encountered some of the amazement Brother Noah did when "the kit" arrived to complete the ark!

Construction was soon underway, and in no time *The Country Church* had another new home. The new building was occupied on August 11, 2002. This facility, though larger, still holds its country charm and continues to use country decor.

The auditorium is in the center of the building with classrooms around the perimeter. Plans are for a small bookstore to be housed in this facility. Bibles, Christian books, and all Christian materials will be sold at cost price. We hope to see much of this Christian material trickle out into the community.

The building itself is of colored metal construction. While *The Country Church* felt this was the most economical form of construction it is interesting to note that few associations, state and national conventions are open to building this type of structure. Architects are reluctant to use it as well because their fees would be minimal. Regardless of what others think about it, this building works wonderfully for us and our need to accommodate the ever growing flock.

When the matter of stewardship arises we evaluated several growing churches in our area. One completed a 900-seat auditorium for $4 million; another 1,200-seat auditorium for over $7 million. It became obvious a 1,100-seat auditorium of *The Country Church* for $650,000 would be a good example of stewardship. It would allow us to focus on winning the lost and making disciples, as opposed to building a more ornate birdbath.

The building continues with the "Country" decor and was occupied August 11, 2002.

In 2004, a 7,000-square-foot children's building was added to the campus. This has provided much needed space for a growing Sunday school. It also allows for the remodeling of our two-year-old auditorium. By eliminating six perimeter classrooms and a portion of the hallways from the auditorium, it will allow us to increase seating by 500 to 600 for the minimal price of $50 to $60,000.

An additional 1,500-square-foot modular building has been added to accommodate our growing benevolent ministry, "The Attic." This ministry is fully staffed by volunteers from our super senior saints.

The church is seeking to purchase four to eight more acres of land from adjoining property owners for future ministry expansion. Here we grow again!

Chapter 11

The Facts

The following is statistical data on *The Country Church* of Marion, Texas, population 1,099.

No attempts are made to parallel progress with any plan of man, but rather to give glory to the lovely Lord Jesus who has truly brought a miracle to Marion.

The following graphs merely chronicle the moving of the precious Holy Spirit in a small South Texas community. While the pastor and the people praise the Lord for the positive, upward trend of these charts, we realize, recognize, and give glory to the one and only Savior who has made it all possible.

If at any time the pastor, staff, or the people of *The Country Church* attempt to share in the glory which belongs to Jesus, please invert these graphs as this will indicated what deserves to happen, a downward spiral. We seek to remember: *"In the Beginning, God Created...The Country Church."*

March 1998 – September 2004
Church Year October 1ˢᵗ thru September 30ᵗʰ

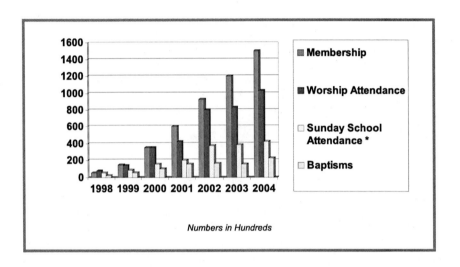

Numbers in Hundreds

	1998	1999	2000	2001	2002	2003	2004
Membership	50	149	344	608	936	1205	1500
Worship Attendance	75	140	358	430	770	829	1025
Sunday School Attendance *	48	80	144	187	231	381	425
Baptisms	20	50	101	153	154	155	224

*Note that Sunday School growth was impeded due to lack of available classroom space and reaching a target group unfamiliar with Sunday School.

Financial (All Receipts)
March 1998 – September 2004
Church Year October 1ˢᵗ thru September 30ᵗʰ

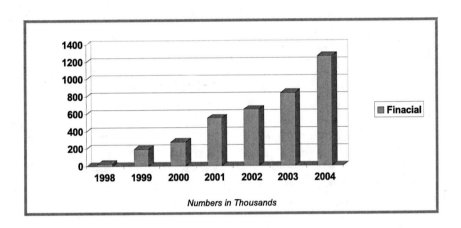

Numbers in Thousands

Total Receipts

1998	1999	2000	2001	2002	2003	2004
$ 85,084.83	$ 306,817.65	$ 371,589	$ 564,919	$ 707,519	$ 839,309	$ 1,266,670

Chapter 12

The Future

Since God created *The Country Church* in March of 1998, many miracles have taken place. Most of these miracles have come as precious souls born into the kingdom. Other believers have come along side to assist in the progress. Someone once said "if we catch on fire, others will come to watch us burn."

As we look to the future, "our eye is on the sky." We believe our Lord Jesus could come at any time, and it is our desire to be found faithful when He comes. What all does that entail?

Facility-wise we need to accommodate those that the Lord is sending and adding to the church. At present we can facilitate 1,100 in worship, seat approximately 700 in Bible study, and can accommodate parking for 505 cars - mostly pickups and Suburbans (the cowboy Cadillac). Our people to vehicle ratio is 2.4 people per vehicle. This figure is recorded each week with other vital statistics and trends.

One of our most practical ventures was birthed as we met in the old tavern. As crowds grew, the small dance floor/bar area would not house the increasing crowds. One of our trustees suggested a camcorder video feed to a TV screen in the pool-room! As visitors came in, our people moved to the side rooms with TV hookups. Was this an ideal set-up? No, but where else can you gain seating for 30 people for $200? This concept was improved upon and carried over into the next two building projects. A third project of this type is on the drawing board should God continue to send the miracle to Marion, Texas.

Investments like this have allowed *The Country Church* to test numerical trends without prematurely adding buildings.

When one looks at pure stewardship, multiple worship and Sunday schools services appear to be the answer. This has worked well for many churches in high-growth areas. However, many of these are in urban areas where "shift-work" is the norm rather than the exception. This author, in a previous rural church, followed this path as the one of least resistance. It was a lesson in assuming "God has said," when in fact, "God had not said!" We followed a trend rather than the Holy Spirit of God.

Case in point, at times in growing churches the suggestion comes from pastor or pew that we move to two services. The pastor comes before the body and asks for some of the committed Christians to sacrifice by attending the early morning service, thereby making room in the second service for visitors. And the committed respond.

Several differences are soon noticed. One, the faithful meet few of the new people because few new people come to the early service. Two, the early service atmosphere becomes a "teaching service" rather than a "reaching service."

Three, the choir and special music have problems hitting the high notes in early morning services. Having music people doing double duty brings its own set of difficulties.

Four, less visitors in early services results in less decisions for Christ. The faithful have less of an air of expectancy of seeing souls saved, Believers baptized, and the church added unto.

Meanwhile, back at the ranch, regular service continues to flourish. Numbers increase, services are enhanced, people are responding to the invitation, and now a decision must be reached about building! A vote is scheduled to be taken.

Remember the committed saints who attended early services? What is now their input? "We don't need to build, there is still room in early service. Let them make the same sacrifices we did!" Each church must seek the leadership of the Holy Spirit in matters such as this rather than yield to a "cookie-cutter" type of church where one size/plan fits all.

Years ago in a Bible conference at Criswell College, Dr. Jerry Falwell made this statement to the pastors attending, "Gentlemen pick your battles, and spit at the others on your way by!" This is one area I would like to spit at while passing.

Because of my grocery marketing background, I view our denomination as a group of successful, independent grocers - each one sensitive to his trade area and adapting to needs to insure future growth. Other church groups prefer the chain store, cookie-cutter approach, where merchandising and marketing is left up to corporate headquarters.

It would do us all well to pause and pray, seeking the Lord's leadership in decision making rather than implementing a plan to insure growth where one size fits all. This author, while loving his denomination, sees it as the buffet line at the local cafeteria where the food is found in more abundance than one can ingest or digest. One should select carefully, trying not to overload the plate yet maintain the goal. Enough said!

Our existing church facilities can be expanded to accommodate 1,600 people plus an additional 250 in an overflow area equipped with large screen televisions. However, additional land must be secured for parking, youth activities, and educational space that would be eliminated by enlarging the auditorium.

The question is, how much land is enough? We can "get all we can and can the rest." Or we can adopt the slogan that "land is something the good Lord is not making anymore of!" As this decision rises in importance, our prayer is that God would give us wisdom as we exercise stewardship.

Educational space will provided through the construction of a two-story facility specially designed for youth and adults. In regards to youth, it is interesting to note what was volleyball, basketball, and baseball, several years ago is now being challenged by soccer, roller blading, skateboarding, and game rooms. This presents creative challenges as we seek to win today's youth.

All of this brings us back to the reason for building, growing, and expanding - that is, and must remain, reaching one more soul for Christ.

Having spent 15 years in sales and marketing, one thing became remarkably clear: nothing happens until someone sells something! Transportation is not a concern, nor is warehouse personnel, bookkeeping, or computer support. In much the same manner, Christendom is advanced by the, saving of a single soul. How do we accomplish the task?

It is this author's opinion that many of our churches are following a dangerous trend. We are looking for one or two successful weeks (in some cases days) to meet our soul-winning responsibilities. Bring someone in to preach heaven down and bring baptisms up! Our people are programmed to seeing salvation as an annual or perhaps a semi-annual event, as opposed to the Lord adding daily to the church those that were being saved.

Another pitfall is our "numbers game." We hire "holy hit men" to reach the lost. Since few churches have a fresh prospect file, and no time is set aside for soul, winning visitation, we resort to other means.

How about dinner every night, and a cardboard pizza bash for the youth? What about chicken parts wieners for the kids? We wind up with overweight bodies and underfed souls!

Now, with no lost in the audience, and the speaker's reputation at stake, what is left to do? How about causing every deacon and Sunday school teacher to doubt their salvation? That will bring some down, we can baptize them again, and tell God we had a great revival!

The Country Church seeks to use major events for the purpose of reaching one more for Christ. This includes drama such as Heaven's Gates/Hell's Flames, rodeo events, and country cookouts. However, these are not to take the place of "as you go evangelism." The reason, many times, that nothing takes place on Sunday, is that nothing has taken place Monday through Saturday.

Luke 10:1-2 gives the church valuable insight.

"After these things the Lord appointed other seventy also, and sent them two and two before his face into every city and place, whither he himself would come. Therefore said he unto them, The harvest truly is great, but the labourers are few: pray ye therefore the Lord of the harvest, that he would send forth labourers into his harvest."

The Greek rendering for "send forth" is literally to "thrust out."

This point was vividly manifested to me by a scene on my own front porch. We have been blessed (tongue-in-check) with that which we refer to as "mud swallows." These feathered friends are bent on proliferating the bird population on the *Lazy I* ranch! My wife will not allow them to be hosed down or disposed of. We wait for the hatching, the feeding, and some distant day, the flight of said creatures from their mud kingdom, or nest.

As I have watched this process repeatedly, several things have come to light. One, the parents do everything in their power to encourage the offspring to leave the nest. Two, the ones who are reluctant to leave "mess up the nest." Three, the bird that refuses to leave the comfort of the nest ultimately dies there. All that remains is stench and dry bones!

Could this be what our Lord conveyed when he used the term "thrust out?"

The Country Church has no future if we do not continue to evangelize. Again, as Dr. Adrian Rogers so ably expressed it, "We evangelize or we fossilize." Visitation must remain a vital part of the pulpit as well as the pew. Every effort must be made to "be church" rather than "play church." Every effort will be made to build the base of Jerusalem so that Judea, Samaria, and the uttermost parts of the will be reached.

I have seen churches where every sacrifice was made to reach Judea, Samaria, and the uttermost to the neglect of Jerusalem. The church oftentimes gave as much as 48 percent of its gross income - much of went to bird baths, atriums, jogging trails, and a meditation lake. All the while, Jerusalem lived with gravel parking lots and storefront classrooms. Every church must pray for balance and stewardship of mission dollars expended.

The Country Church seeks to multiply its witness through the planting of New Testament Churches. Through prayer and experience, we feel that these should be 20 to 30 miles from the sponsoring church. Due to the uniqueness of this ministry, people have a tendency to drive from further distances. Because of the absence of committee structures, strong leadership, personal soul-winning, and financial understanding is a must for *The Country Church* planter.

While *The Country Church* has become identified by the cowboy kneeling at the cross, it is not to be confused with the cowboy church movement which often meets in arenas with preaching prior to rodeo events. Their facilities oftentimes consist of a metal barn, covered arena, and hay bales for pews. *The Country Church* has had inquires from these evangelistic fellowships as they seek to become functional churches. We see this as further potential to reach the unchurched for Christ.

In many ways God has taken the "Cowboy Fellowship" far beyond the original vision. Should this happen to your ministry, nurseries, classrooms, buildings, budgets, or Bible studies, and increased structure is needed, *The Country Church* can serve as a model without moving to *"First Church"* status.

Another field that God has placed before us is the ever growing Hispanic community in South Texas. The mission field is coming to us. In our community there is a Country-Tejano mix that relates to *The Country Church* atmosphere, which reaches out to the unchurched male. In many Latin cultures, church has been for mama and the kids.

In many of our southern cities we have observed a "white flight." We see not only an exodus of families, but of evangelistic churches as well. Our prayer is that God will use us in these uncharted waters.

Last, but not least, is the need to raise the visibility of the church. This is being done through an ever increasing plan of advertising and marketing. A dear friend, Dr. Ray Davis of Tyler, Texas, wrote his dissertation on "Marketing the Church in Today's Society."

The Country Church sees tremendous potential in using radio and television to reach the unchurched. In "fishing" where the fish are, TV advertising spots are likely to be used during programs such as wrestling, "Movies For Guys Who Like Movies" on TNT, monster truck competition and other "guy friendly shows. Radio advertising will continue to focus on country-western spots designed to reach the unchurched male.

The future is here. Opportunity is knocking. The door is open, and we must go through it.

Conclusion

During a recent visit with Paige Patterson, we had the opportunity to discuss the progress of this particular work. A few weeks after our meeting, Dr. Patterson wrote me regarding something that later came to his mind. Upon reading his letter, I began to sense God was speaking to me about one more thing that needed to be a part of this book.

In that subsequent letter, Dr. Patterson wrote of his thoughts regarding how so many of the simple, yet innovative concepts applied at

The Country Church could be "transferred" to other churches praying about new ways to reach and disciple people. He said that not only could they be applied in other places and ministries, he suggested that they should be!

We all agree that it is unreasonable to think that every single thing we do at *The Country Church* will work everywhere. No doubt some of our ideas would go over like a lead balloon elsewhere. But many of the things we do here will work for those in the right situation.

Having a business background, I can tell you from experience that the business and communication worlds both teach of transferable concepts. Some of the things we do here at *The Country Church* will not work in your setting – they are not transferable. Other things are of such great consequence that I believe they are transferable anywhere to the benefit of the church.

Some concepts will be transferable especially to similar types of church plants. Below I want to summarize these ideas in no particular order. Of course, the lists, though they may be exhausting, are not exhaustive.

The first set of transferable concepts are gleaned from the New Testament and will work anywhere. It is my belief that everyone planting a new church, or reforming an old one, must include these ministries. In fact, I would go so far as to say you do not even need to pray about doing these things. Certainly pray as you do them to, but you don't have pray about whether or not you should make them a part of your ministry. The Master said do 'em, so let's get busy doin' 'em.

Prayer	There is no way to accurately articulate the power of a praying church. So why are so many churches weak and dying? Jesus said, *"My Father's house shall be a house of prayer..."* In the American church today, prayer is now an afterthought. There is so much I could say about prayer, but I will simply say for the sake of brevity, if you are a church planter and prayer is not primary, throw this book away and go do something else. Without prayer you will fail, even if you do somehow manage to draw a crowd.
Evangelism	People forget the first part of the great commission — the *"all authority is given unto me"* part. It was after that when Jesus said *"Go"* make me some disciples. Friends, my question is, "Who gave you the authority not to go?" Winning one more person to Christ must be the passion of the church planter. You be a soul-winner and lead others to be soul-winners too. And tell yourself over and over, "All I need to grow a great church is Jesus and lost people, and both are everywhere."
Preaching	"Preach the word; be instant in season, out of season; reprove, rebuke, exhort with all longsuffering and doctrine." Guys, save the pop-psychology for the coffee shop. If it ain't in *The Book*, you don't need to say it when you're preaching. Just stand up very prepared, read the passage, explain it, apply it, illustrate it, call hearers to respond, then sit down and hush. Of course, do it in a way that is interesting, passionate, relevant, and memorable. And if you have the spiritual gift of humor, use it.
Worship	Weekly, God-centered, Christ-exalting worship is absolutely necessary if you want God's hand of blessing on your life and work. I am not talking about creating the best show in town. I am talking about creating an atmosphere and service where people get to spend about an hour and a half in the presence of God, honoring and adoring the Savior. Please, please, please...if it does not bring glory and honor to God, leave it out.
Fellowship	Get your people together often. It sounds crazy, but get them together once a week, if possible, or at the least once a month to share a meal together. The early church ate together all the time! There was a good reason then and there still is. We need each other, and we need more time together than just a couple of hours on Sundays. Work to provide that time. Wednesday night suppers

	are excellent. They do more than just make it easier for people to get to church for mid-week service. It provides them with much needed Christian fellowship. Have special events throughout the year where folks get together just to enjoy one another. You get them together and watch God the Holy Spirit knit their hearts together in a way that makes church-fussing a thing of the past.
Baptism and The Lord's Supper	Jesus said to do both — 'nuff said.
Discipleship	As a church planter your passion is to reach people for Christ. I am with you there. But let me encourage you to be faithful at discipling those that come to Jesus. Fulfill all three parts of the Great Commission, not just the first two. After you win them and baptize them, spend some energy "teaching them to observe all things." If necessary, humble yourself and be honest with yourself that your passion is winning souls not discipling converts. It is not a sin to admit that. What is a sin is winning them and then letting them go through life a powerless and undiscipled Believer. If you need to call an associate pastor to help get discipling done, do it! Just do what you must to move them from the milk to the meat.
Stewardship	Every congregation must pray fervently about how to be a great steward over the finances of the church. Be diligent in financial matters and use biblical commands and precepts to determine your course. Do not be afraid to preach and teach on financial matters. Teach and encourage the people to put God to the test. Teach them to tithe, trust them to do it, and watch God pour out so much blessing there will not be room enough for it.
Mercy Ministries	Jesus seemed to spend most of His time with hurting, needy people. Never forget that He is not just our Master, but also our model. Do the things necessary to care for the needs of those truly needy people around you. Establish policies, be prudent, be firm, be cautious, but most of all, be willing to meet physical needs. As you do, keep in mind two things: one, when you are caring for people's needs, they will usually listen to you as you share Jesus two, when you are caring for the hurting, you are doing service to our Master "Whatsoever you do unto the least of these…"

Pastoral Leadership	During my years in evangelism, I spoke with hundreds of church members who were not happy with their pastor – not because he was not a good preacher, but because he was passive and not a good leader. Regardless of where you have come down on the issues related to elder, deacon, or congregational rule, you cannot get around the fact that as a pastor/planter, God has given you a very unique, very significant role in leading His people. You cannot just preach well to be a great pastor. You must lead. Do not be lazy and do not be overbearing. Do not fear man or myth. Preach the Word as it. The Word instructs church members to *"Obey them that have rule over you."* And remember, the sheep will follow a shepherd who consistently loves, protects, and feeds them.

This second list contains concepts that have been adopted at *The Country Church* which, though perhaps not applicable everywhere, would certainly be applicable to other similar church planting efforts. Keep in mind we are "country folk" and a lot of what we do is based upon who we are. If the people you are trying to reach and disciple don't know who Hank Williams, Jr. is, some of these may not work for you.

Milk Cans	As mentioned above, giving tithes and offerings is biblical, God-exalting, and necessary. But nothing in the Scriptures says you must incorporate into every service a time to "pass the plates." Trust God's people to be obedient to give. Provide a convenient, practical way for the people to give as they come and go to worship.
Hatracks, Harley Parking, and Dually Space	Know your people and provide things that make them feel wanted and loved. Our congregation here is made up of people from every facet of life—different ages, different vocations, different hobbies, and different views on life. But the one thing most everyone has in common is that we are all just plain ole country folk—we live out in the country. So, we didn't install stained glass, chandeliers, and an organ in our sanctuary. Instead, our church is equipped racks for cowboy hats and milk cans for the offering. An old saddle, a spoked-wheel wagon, and quilts on the wall for dÈcor add to the warm country feel. Outside there are swing sets, barbeque pits, picnic tables, and places to park both motorcycles and dually pickups. It seems strange, but these are the people whom God has sent our way. It is who we are, and we have made a place where people can come and be who they are.

Multi-purpose Buildings	With economical metal buildings that have suspended ceilings, alterations can be made with minimal expense. For example, we recently enlarged auditorium by 400 seats for $40,000.
Bi-vocational Pastoral Staff	There are several reasons to consider bi-vocational staff. For us, the number one reason is that we would rather have more coverage of ministry for the dollar invested. For example, we may employ three staff members for the same dollar amount as one full-time staff member would typically cost (including salary, benefits and health insurance). This staffing method also allows a person to concentrate on their area of expertise. Too often, churches hire someone in a "dual-roll" position who has only a passion in one of the areas for which he was hired. In other words, we tell the music minister that if he really wants the job, he has to be the youth director, too. Most of the time, that is insensitive and cruel-both to the minister of music and to the teenagers.
Excellent Administrative Staff	Let's be honest about this one. The brains of almost every operation is the secretary – and that is definitely true in churches. In fact, a church secretary can make or break a pastor. Be careful that you don't hire administrative staff based upon sentiment. Pray about it, and at the same time apply very sound business sense to this decision. Find bright, experienced, hardworking administrative staff and do what you must to keep the great ones. Recognize their contribution to the success of your ministry and reward them for it.
Reach Men	Focus on reaching husbands and fathers for Christ. You have heard it before, and I can tell you from experience it is true. When you win a man to Christ, you will win his family. The Bible says, "He that winneth souls is wise." I tell you, brothers, win men and watch God show how He rewards wisdom. *The Country Church* is filled with men bringing their families to church.
No Committees	I saw a sign that said, "If Moses would have formed committees, the Hebrews would still be in Egypt." Take an honest look folks - there are no committees in the Bible. Just Godly men leading Godly men to live and do the will of God. Be the leader God called you to be and surround yourself with wise, biblically qualified counselors (elders and deacons). The people will follow you as you follow Christ.

Public Invitations	There is much criticism of the public invitation. I agree there are reasons to be critical of some forms of the invitations given today. But many do not give an invitation at all and others just "stand up front and hope something happens." Jesus said publicly, "Come unto me all ye that are weary..." AND THEY CAME! He cried out publicly, "If you are thirsty, COME and drink." I am not talking about appealing to the congregation's flesh or playing on their emotions. I am talking about standing up front and publicly saying, "COME TO CHRIST." They will come.
Sunday Night Events	At our church, we do not have a regularly scheduled Sunday night worship service. This has turned out to be such a blessing as we now have a time available for special events. At first we did not have Sunday night service because I was still in evangelism when we started *The Country Church*. But now that I am here all the time, we keep Sunday nights open so we can use that for baptisms, fellowships, concerts, and other special services. Something great always happens on the Sunday nights we do meet. And besides, when you baptize about 30 people a month, it takes a whole service. For us, that is always a Sunday night. So for our people, Sunday night is always a treat – not a chore. And that is what I pray for you, too.
Thursday Night Mid-week Services	Most revivals today last from Sunday evening through Wednesday night. So, for the same reason we did not originally have a Sunday night service, we couldn't have one on Wednesday night either. But having a mid-week service is very important. God's people need the mid-week encouragement. So we decided to have our mid-week service on Thursday nights. And it works great! We have a fellowship meal together and then head to the worship center for a full-blown worship event. We sing, preach, pray, give, and lead people to Jesus just like on Sunday morning. It is an exciting time, and the people come. It is what fits best with our folks. Perhaps Tuesday or Wednesday night will work best for you. Just be sure to have one, and make it a day that is most helpful to your people.

Conclusion

And Finally

This pastor/planter has been truly blessed. Saved by our Lord and Savior Jesus Christ. Surrendered to service by the call of the Almighty God and the wooing of His precious Holy Spirit, in response to his infallible Word.

Blessed for over 40 years with the bride of my youth, "Mrs. Joanie." Given children which are a heritage of the Lord: son, Keith and wife Annette Ikels; daughter, Melissa and husband Mark Stough. Grandchildren that are the crown of an old man: Derrick, Kristie, Danyelle, Amber, and Nathan.

Thankful to the saints at Salem Sayers Baptist church in Adkins, Texas, who gave an ignorant and unlearned young preacher a chance, and put up with him for over 15 years!

Appreciative to the numerous small churches and saints who supported and sustained us for five years in evangelism.

Indebted to the saints of *The Country Church* of Marion, Texas, who make up "The Miracle at Marion." Real people with real problems, yet not an ounce of plastic in any of them, those to whom we have been blessed "to ride the river with."

Enriched by real friends in the faith - friends who have prayed for this pastor, loved him in spite of his faults, and continued to encourage him over this journey.

Burdened that one more might find Jesus sweet to his soul. If God would be pleased to grant this pastor's request, it would be that I would be holding two lost people' hands, praying the sinner's prayer when the rapture takes place!

Challenged by Godly men like Dr. Richard Wells, former president of Criswell College, Dr. Allan Streett, professor of evangelism at Criswell College, and Dr. Paige Patterson, President of Southwestern Baptist Theological Seminary to record "The Miracle at Marion.

Praying that God would use these simple notations to encourage and inspire one more pastor to plant a work for the glory of our Savoir, the Lord Jesus.

Convicted and encouraged by I Corinthians 1:18-31, as we press on toward the mark for the prize of the high calling of God in Christ Jesus. (Philippians 3:14)

Indebted,

Elton "Butch" Ikels
Pastor/Planter
"In the Beginning God Created...The Country Church"